UNDERCOVER PROP

UNDERCOVER PROP

The game they play in heaven and a police career from hell

DAN CROWLEY

MACMILLAN
Pan Macmillan Australia

Wallaby Gold: The History of Australian Test Rugby by Peter Jenkins and Matthew Alvarez
Published in 1999
Reprinted by permission of Random House Australia
Thanks to Wayne Smith of the *Courier-Mail* and the *Sunday Mail*, Andrew Dawson of
the *Courier-Mail*, and Gordon Bray for permission to reproduce their work.

First published 2005 in Macmillan by Pan Macmillan Australia Pty Limited
St Martins Tower, 31 Market Street, Sydney

National Library of Australia
Cataloguing-in-Publication data:

Crowley, Dan.
Undercover prop: the game they play in heaven and a police career from hell.

ISBN 1 40503676 1.

1. Crowley, Dan. 2. Rugby Union football players – Australia – Biography.
3. Police – Queensland – Biography. 4. Undercover operations – Queensland.
I. Writer, Larry. II. Title.

796.3338092

Typeset in 13/16 pt AGaramond by Post Pre-press Group
Printed in Australia by McPherson's Printing Group

Papers used by Pan Macmillan Australia Pty Ltd are natural, recyclable products
made from wood grown in sustainable forests. The manufacturing processes
conform to the environmental regulations of the country of origin.

To Mum and Dad, for your guidance and love. To my loving wife, Lisa, without whose love and support I would not have achieved half of what I have; and to my children, Jessie, Maddie, Chaise and Tom, you are just so beautiful.

And finally, to the policemen and policewomen who risk their lives every day, thank you.

CONTENTS

INTRODUCTION

'KEEP LOOKING AT THE NEEDLE, don't turn away, don't flinch, keep looking at the needle,' I tell myself as the person sitting beside me in the passenger seat of my Lite Ace van attempts for the second time to find a suitable vein, before sticking the long, blunt surgical steel syringe into his left arm. Because, as an undercover policeman, my job is to play the role of a fellow drug taker and dealer, I force myself to watch, to give the man the impression that I had seen and performed the same act myself a thousand times before. The addict's routine. The paranoid fumblings of a person whose only thought is to mix a solution, inject it and go to a world I do not understand nor would ever want to understand.

I watch this man, or the remains of one, carefully unwrap the silver Alfoil package of heroin which he had taken to sample. He exposes his treasure. The white god, *his* god, the one thing that drives him from hour to hour, day to

1

day. Heroin. I watch as he takes a small amount, a quarter the size of your little fingernail, and places it into his self-modified spoon head, blackened from repeated heating and with the handle removed to fit easily into the coin pocket of his jeans. Inexperienced police, he knows, rarely search there.

Now he dribbles spit into the white powder. The syringe, which he has taken from the inside pocket of his jacket, has been used many times. He places it nonchalantly on the seat between us. A master of his craft, he heats the bottom of the spoon with the flame from a cigarette lighter until the spit starts to bubble. Quickly he retrieves the syringe and uses the blunted needle tip to mix the saliva and the heroin into a solution.

While he is preoccupied, I discreetly reach across and grab the small foil wrapper which still contains a couple of grams of white powder. I slip the package, which cost the Queensland Government around $1000, into my pocket.

I watch as, slowly and deliberately, he draws the spoon's contents up into the syringe, ensuring every last droplet of the fluid is trapped. All the time he is glancing around outside the van.

'Keep looking at the needle,' I tell myself. I'm not squeamish, but it's hard to observe what he's doing without flinching. He shoves the blunt needle in, but his flesh only indents, doesn't puncture, under the pressure. Many past puncture marks scar his arm. I watch as he repeats the attempt and this time he succeeds in breaking the skin. The steel point sinks in. He draws back the syringe, and as I struggle to control my revulsion, I see his blood mixing with the contents of the syringe's vial.

Hunched over, below the line of my van's dashboard, he slowly and deliberately depresses the plunger and the fluid disappears into his arm.

Suddenly he jerks bolt upright and arches his back. Then he bends at the middle and slumps towards me into the middle of the front seat. He groans slightly as the wind leaves his body. He collapses, the needle still protruding from his arm. The heroin, smack, the gear, call it any of its many names, was too strong, even for this drug veteran.

'Fuck,' I think, in a panic, 'oh God, oh God, oh God . . . don't die on me! Don't die on me!'

What am I going to do? This can't be happening. An instant hot flush, like a blush of embarrassment, comes over my body. I look out the windscreen of my van and time seems to slow.

Thursday afternoon, mid-January 1987, I am parked on the Gold Coast Highway, the main road through the tourist capital of Australia, just 50 metres from the Chevron Hotel. While this is taking place, there are people walking by not 2 metres away. Parents with children on school holidays, pensioners shopping, businesspeople between meetings.

'Bloody hell, can't you wait till we get somewhere a bit more isolated to shoot up?' I'd said to him earlier. 'Oh, no, no, no, no,' he'd replied, 'I'm hangin'. My mate reckons it's good stuff. You in?' Yeah, I told him, but I said I'd wait because I didn't want to shoot up there.

That's the indiscriminate nature of heroin addiction: one person must have it all the time and straight away; another can do without it from time to time. My new friend was not at all suspicious that I had knocked the heroin back.

His focus was totally on getting it himself: and getting it now.

My mind starts racing. 'What'll I do? Think. Think. The boss is going to fuckin' kill me! Call the ambulance? No. Doctor? No. What if he's dead? I'll dump him, no one will know. Should I just roll him out into the gutter and drive off?'

Twenty years old with no medical training, I am in a world of trouble. My new friend is too. I turn his head to face me and pull back his right eyelid expecting to see his pupil. What stares back at me is a film of cloudy white. His eyeball has rolled back in its socket. I begin shaking him, slapping his face. I don't know what I am doing. I pull the syringe out of his arm and throw it onto the floor of the cab. I splash the contents of a bottle of soft drink all over his face. I don't know what I am doing but it is better than doing nothing.

At last, after about a minute, he starts to moan and slowly moves his head. I pull him up by the shirt and lean him against the passenger window, and buckle him in so he doesn't flop forward. I start the van and drive south towards his home. I think that once I get there I can work this out. At least he's not dead. As we drive through Surfers Paradise I keep looking at him, dribbling from the corner of his mouth, head wobbling, babbling. He's alive. I'm safe.

Ten minutes later I turn into the driveway of his rented single-storey, two-bedroom fibro house. Inside is his wife, also an addict, and their four-year-old son. By this time he is lucid.

'You scared the living shit out of me,' I tell him.

'Hey,' he says slowly, '*that* is really, really good smack. You are going to have to make sure you cut it up or someone will drop. Can I take some more?'

'Get rooted,' I reply. 'You've had your taste. I've gotta go. I'll catch you later tonight.'

As I begin the hour's drive to Brisbane, my nerves start to settle. Four months of undercover work nearly dead in the seat beside me and I wasn't yet at the halfway point of the investigation. 'This is one I won't tell the boss about for a while,' I think.

The fellow who nearly overdosed was a local dealer, but connected to the drug importer who was my quarry. It had taken me three months to get near him and it was our second deal. I knew that by rescuing him from overdosing I had cemented our relationship, and he now trusted me. He trusted me enough to introduce me to others and that was my responsibility as an undercover policeman. Gain their trust, be one of them, eat, sleep, walk, talk, live like one of them. Find the main source of who trafficked the heroin and gather the evidence to have them arrested.

In 1987, Queensland Government legislation stated that anyone trafficking in heroin received a mandatory life sentence. The same sentence applied for murder. If the undercover police officer was the only one with the evidence to convict a criminal, he or she would very likely eliminate the cop to get rid of the evidence. It was a chance worth taking. Mandatory life is mandatory life – no matter why you're serving it.

Although that was always in the back of my mind, I drove into the Souths car park that day for rugby training, straight from my afternoon drug deal. As I parked the van, I leaned down and retrieved the needle that only an hour or so before came so close to taking a life. I opened the glove box, threw the syringe inside and closed it. I was smiling, knowing that I was getting closer to the importer.

1

A BRISBANE BOY

A REPORTER ONCE WROTE a feature article about me when I was playing rugby for Queensland or Australia and had gotten myself into trouble for belting some bloke. I can't remember who the journalist was, but it doesn't matter now. The feature was headlined 'The Hard Case'. Fair enough, I suppose. If you're a soft case you don't become a Wallaby prop forward, an undercover cop or an investigator, all of which I've been. But to me, 'being hard' is not about whether you can stand toe to toe with any opponent in life, it's about whether you are mentally tough enough to be the best you can be at whatever you do.

My mother and father were born in Liverpool, England, home of the Beatles, though I don't think Dad was really into pop music and, anyway, he and Mum emigrated to Australia in the mid-1950s, before John, Paul, George and Ringo got big in the early '60s. But even had the Beatles been around, playing at the Cavern or some other Liverpudlian dive, knowing Dad, I doubt that he would have paid the money to get in the door.

Being a little too young to fight in World War II, Dad served in the army and was involved in the mop-up after 1945. He did his fighting with gloves on. He boxed a bit, in and out of the ring. Mum told me had a fair temper in his younger days. I have a sneaking suspicion he may have approved of the way I didn't back down in my rugby days, but he's cooled down now. Age has mellowed my father.

Dad is an old-fashioned bloke. His family didn't have much, like many in the war era, so he and Mum have been careful with money all their lives. He left school at 10 or 11 to go to work, and from then on looked after his own education. He knows what he knows, which is a lot, by reading every book he's ever been able to lay his hands on. All his life he's read and read and read. Even today, at age 77, he and Mum always have their noses in a book.

In Liverpool, Dad was a truck driver, a hard worker and a loyal employee who drove for the same company for many years. When he and Mum arrived in Australia they spent time at Miles in central Queensland, an area far removed physically, culturally and every other way possible from the north of England. About the only thing they have in common is that central Queensland and England's north breed tough, down-to-earth people. In the Queensland outback, even while he was battling terrible homesickness and loneliness — at first he didn't know a soul out there — Dad worked long and hard hours at whatever labouring work came his way. A year or so later, he and Mum moved to the south side of Brisbane, where they settled and bought a house. That house is the very same one they live in today. They're very solid people. If any of the mates I grew up with ever want to find me these days they go straight to Mum and Dad's, and they put them on my trail.

Dad started driving trucks again, picking up from where he left off in the streets of Liverpool. After a few years finding his feet, he found a company he liked to work for and drove for them for 30 years transporting food and alcohol all around Brisbane.

Throughout my life, Mum has been the unsung hero, always in the background working to ensure that the family stayed on track. She, like many mothers, is the glue that binds us and the foundation for our family's success. Being a truck driver, Dad wasn't on big money, so for much of my life Mum worked to provide the little extras and looked after the family. Talk about mental toughness. She is a rock.

We're a close family, but somehow my parents and I have never really talked too much about their history. I do know that they saw no great future for themselves in England after they married. Even so, it must have been a huge decision for them to leave all of their family and friends behind in Liverpool and re-establish themselves in faraway Australia. They've only been back to England once, to see me play in the 1991 Rugby World Cup. When he arrived in Liverpool, Dad gave the city a quick once-over, and turned to Mum and said, 'Hmmph, now you know why we left.' After all those years in Brisbane, they could no longer stand the cold. You could see a slight sadness in both of them that the city where they grew up had become run-down. It was sad for them to see the urban decay. Unemployment had soared and bred boredom that in turn caused the vandalism that marred the city. Liverpool was always a worker's town, some would say rough, but there was always something happening there. It's a place where my parents made many memories. They were going to travel to Leeds when I had a season with the Leeds Tykes late in my career, but by then Dad had developed a heart condition and emphysema and doctors warned him not to fly.

For the record, I was born at the Royal Brisbane Women's Hospital on 28 August 1965. That makes me 39. I'm the youngest of five children. Sadly, the first-born, twins, a girl and a boy, died shortly after they were born. Then Mum and Dad had Michael in 1958 and Martin in 1961. Michael grew up to become a very good policeman. Martin became a very good builder, and a drug addict.

Memories? Some people have total recall of their past and can provide names, dates and serial numbers at the drop of a hat. Not me, or so I thought for a long time. My life prior to yesterday always seemed like a blank. I put it down to a bad memory, a short attention span, or all those times I was whacked in the head when I was playing football. On occasions I think, 'Am I going down the road of Muhammad Ali?', the great boxer who now has dementia from the blows he sustained. But I don't think so. Not yet, anyway. Apart from really important stuff, like remembering lineout calls and never losing track of my cover stories when, as a policeman, I'd have to pass myself off as a drug dealer (forgetting the yarns I'd made up about my life could have proved fatal), I'd tend to live in the moment, the moment would pass, and I'd be on to the next thing. People tell me the older you get the more important to you your past becomes. Maybe what they say makes sense – I certainly got a shock when I was writing this book. It's been great mental discipline. Forcing myself to revisit the past has been good therapy and memories of many incidents that I'd not thought about for decades, things that I've locked away in some mental reservoir, have come flooding back.

I'm a stable, steady sort of bloke, and I thank Mum and Dad for that. They laid a solid platform. I've never really lived more than 15 kilometres from the family home where I grew up. I'm comfortable with that. Rugby has given me the chance to travel all over the world, and I love being overseas, but being in Brisbane with its climate, natural beauty, decent people and opportunities, I truly believe that I live in one of the best places on Earth. I figure that if I've found that, and know it and give thanks for it every single day, why would I want to live anywhere else? I think sometimes people don't appreciate what they've got and go away looking fruitlessly for things and experiences as rewarding as those they actually already have in their own backyard. My dream is to give my kids the solid platform and sense of security that Mum and Dad gave me.

I know stability isn't a guarantee that the rest of your life is going to be smooth sailing. My brother Martin is evidence of that. And I've met so many kids and adults from ugly, violent and unstable backgrounds who are the best people you'd ever come across. But knowing that you're loved, and there's food on the table and a roof over your head, gives you a bloody good head start.

We grew up in the Catholic faith, going to church every Sunday, and, as a kid, from grade one to grade three, I attended St Elizabeth Convent School, where, I'm sorry to confess, I learned to hate the nuns. A vast majority were brutal, and believed that the rod would rectify behaviour and teach discipline. The cane was their weapon of choice. They seemed to enjoy flogging us. Eat a sandwich in the wrong part of the playground, and they'd beat you. Talk in class, and they'd beat you. Look left instead of right, and they'd beat you. I admit I was by no means the most angelic kid in the school and that I enjoyed goading these women as they'd beat me, and then I'd go out of my way to be even more badly behaved. For any seven to 10 year old, being caned leaves an indelible mark on their young mind.

I don't know if my day-to-day war with the nuns had an adverse effect on my studies, but I was only a 50 per cent student. I do know I didn't enjoy schoolwork and didn't try too hard.

After grade three I said a not-so-heartfelt farewell to my holy tormentors at St Elizabeth's, and went to St Laurence's College, South Brisbane, an all-boys' school. It was daunting there after tiny St Elizabeth's. What I didn't realise was that I had swapped the Catholic nuns for the Catholic brothers. And the cane for the strap. These blokes also hit harder than the nuns. I tried hard to establish myself in a school that had more than a thousand boys. I was fortunate in one sense that I had two older brothers at St Laurence's who knew the ropes, but unfortunate in another in that they and their friends had fresh meat to try their schoolyard pranks on. Michael, being the oldest, was basically a normal student. He would get into trouble on occasions but in general he kept his head below the radar. Martin, on the other hand, flew so far above the radar he needed an oxygen mask. He was constantly in strife. We three boys have a little saying from our youth: 'Michael did things wrong and got away with it. Martin did things wrong and always got caught. Dan did things wrong and confessed.' This saved me the hassle of trying not to get caught and, because I gave myself up, often the punishment wasn't as bad.

In my first year at St Elizabeth's, in grade one, I met three guys, Adam McDonald, Craig Senior, and Andrew Johnstone, and we became the best of mates. I still see a lot of Adam, who was best man when my wife and I got married, and Craig. We four were inseparable right through school and for a couple of years after, then Johnno just drifted away. He took up with a different crowd who were into drugs. I didn't know how deeply Johnno was into it and didn't want to know. Johnno's new mates weren't my sort of crowd and I left him be. Adam and Craig and I were more into footy. On the rare occasions when Johnno and I ran into each other, we'd say, 'How are you, mate? What's going on?' I would invite him over for a barbeque but he wouldn't show. We drifted apart and weren't close friends anymore. Drugs do many bad things, and one of them is that they strain great friendships. About seven years after Johnno left school he came off the back of a motorbike and became a paraplegic. He died three or so years ago from the complications of his disability. Johnno had a great talent as a painter and signwriter, he had great parents and a loving family. It was a sad waste of a good, decent bloke. I look back now and wonder was there something more that I could have done to help Johnno, but the opportunity, like the spent arrow, has gone.

It was Adam and Craig who got me playing rugby, at St Elizabeth's in grade two, in the Under 8s. God knows why. Craig, whose older brothers played football and who lived near Shaftesbury Oval, the home ground of Southern Districts Junior Rugby Union Football Club – or Souths – summed me up. 'You're fat, slow and have no skills. You'll make a terrific prop.' So I began in the front row of the Under 8s where one of my teammates was Peter Slattery, who, as a halfback, became a Wallaby teammate.

Apart from a bit of backyard footy with Adam and Craig and some schoolmates, I'd never played before. My brothers weren't really into football. But I really enjoyed rugby union. It was a game made for blokes like me. In my teen years I played for Souths' junior teams and also for St Laurence's. The school team had first dibs of course, so when there was a clash I'd have to pull out of the Souths sides. In the summer I played school cricket and volleyball. I made a dozen or so friends at St Laurence's whom I consider to be among my very best mates today. As the saying goes, 'Good mates are like good books. You don't need many.'

I reckon we're friends for the same reason I've never strayed far from where I grew up. I gravitate towards stability, and these guys grew up in solid working class families much like mine. No one had a lot of money. Unlike today when careers can take you all over the place, our dads tended to work for the same company all their lives, and most of our mothers juggled part-time jobs with looking after the kids. My parents put their three sons through private school, and made sure we never went without. Dad was always out driving his truck, receiving only the basic wage. Mum did bookkeeping and sold Avon cosmetics door to door to make ends meet and was always there for us kids.

A child with divorced parents was rare. All our parents are getting on in years now, but most live in the same houses as they did when we were kids. Craig's mum moved recently, but only because her husband died. We're all old-school.

No one's family could afford expensive homes, cars or swimming pools, but we played sport together, swam in the local public pool and rode our bikes. There was a forest in our neighbourhood. We played footy Test matches and cricket games that lasted for four days. You went out into the fresh air and made your own fun. TV was terrible, and there were no computers in those less complicated years. We were happier, fitter and healthier, I believe, than modern kids.

The streets were safer, too. We went out to play at 9 o'clock in the morning and wouldn't come home till dark. It's hard to imagine parents letting their kids rumble around in a forest today, or just letting them head off into the park, or down the street. I can't say I blame them. There are more seriously sick and dangerous people out there today than when we were growing up. It's a fact. Paedophiles, drug dealers – blokes who just enjoy hurting others. People who steal because they think the world owes them a living, and they don't have to do a scrap of work if they don't feel like it. There are some very twisted individuals out there, and I speak from experience because I have spent a portion of my life putting them behind bars. I feel so sorry for the children of today who are not getting the chances to have good fun in the outdoors. They are having the wonderful years of childhood taken away from them.

I played every game going, but rugby was my sport. I loved it. I wasn't a worldbeater as a child, but I was OK. I mainly played prop because of my nuggety build, strength and lack of real speed, but because I also had some ball skills, from

15

time to time I'd get picked to play in the centres, at fullback or five-eighth and make a fair enough fist of it. I made the Brisbane Under 13s and Under 14s rep teams, but missed out on the Queensland and Australian schoolboy sides. Apart from any lack of talent, I struggled to overcome two problems. One was that my school, St Laurence's, was an Associated School, and it was the Greater Public Schools, the GPS, that had a stranglehold on selection for the state and national teams. The other was that one of the selectors, renowned coach Alec Evans, thought I was too small to play prop. Even in 1998 and 1999 when I'd played for the Wallabies many, many times, Alec was still telling anyone who'd listen that I was too small. He and others who trumpeted that line of thought made me determined to prove them wrong and give them no choice but to pick me for the team by being stronger and a better scrummager than beefier blokes.

Whether it was a little bit of short-man or fat-kid syndrome, I definitely had a chip on my shoulder in my younger days. Being at a school of just boys, I thought that if you were one of the toughest you were one of the best. So I pushed my short, fat weight around. Winning sometimes, losing at others. Looking back I'm not real proud of the way I acted in certain circumstances. Don't get me wrong, it wasn't as if I went around in a gang and preyed on my schoolmates. It was more that I pushed harder than others who were in my way.

In grade nine, there was a hard-case kid, much bigger than me, who wanted to fight me. Some other boy had said to this bloke, 'Crowley's tougher than you are,' and the hard-case wanted to prove him wrong. Dad had never exactly taught me how to fight, but I guess a bit of technique got passed from father to son. Mainly I just picked up on how to look after myself in a blue, and I was also doing some weights – as I was starting to get keen on football.

Anyway, the kid kept picking on me in the playground. By that time, I'd settled down a lot and wasn't as aggressive as I was when I was younger. I'd just about learned by then that the real tough guys aren't the blokes who go around swaggering and threatening. No, it's the quiet ones with a self-confidence born of a belief that they'll never back down who can really intimidate. I'd developed self-confidence and didn't need to throw my weight around as much anymore. 'Mate, rack off!' I told the tough bloke when he began shoving me around. Then he threw a punch at me, and my self-restraint evaporated. It was on. Kids came running from everywhere as we whaled into each other. Soon teachers had forced their way through the hordes of kids all yelling in unison, in the time-honoured schoolyard tradition, 'Fight! Fight! Fight!' and were trying to pull me off my adversary.

One teacher, Mr Mewing (he's a friend of mine these days), dragged me away and really gave it to me. 'Crowley, you're nothing but a troublemaker! Always going around starting fights!'

If I was mad before, now I lost it totally. I had always been a respectful kid and was deferential to my elders, but Mewing was unjustly accusing me of instigating the brawl. I had been trying hard to stop fighting, but once you have a reputation for something it is hard to get rid of it. 'Bullshit!' I roared at him. This was the first time I'd ever blown up at a teacher. 'Ask any of these kids. I didn't start the fight. I did everything I could not to get involved.' We had a knock 'em down, drag 'em out argument, but it was a real turning point in my maturity.

One of my good mates at St Laurence's was Ian Cameron. Ian has been a friend ever since we got to know each other in grade 11. We had plenty in common, and always have had. Ian was a policeman, still is, and is connected to Souths, where he now coaches A grade. At school we played rugby and cricket together, but when I asked him for some memories for this book, they were not exactly complimentary: 'Dan was a very good opening batsman, but a lousy slips fielder. He once dropped three guys in a single innings off my bowling. St Laurence's staunchest opponent was the neighbouring Villanova Boys' School. A couple of years ago, Villanova invited Dan to be guest at their speech night. First thing Dan did, remembering the old school rivalry, was to get up and thank them for inviting him and then outline how good it was to see that the school had gone co-ed as they had finally got men's toilets. I can't say it went over very well, but no one was going to contradict him, Dan being Dan.'

We had fun, my schoolmates and I. Ian Cameron has another rather embarrassing memory of me when we were 18 and took a South Seas cruise on the liner *Fairstar*: 'Dan was drunk the whole time. In Tonga he bought a huge jigsaw puzzle only so that he would have a bigger jigsaw than anybody else. Being a staunch Queenslander, he insisted that we all drink nothing but Fourex beer while we were onboard. By the end of one day he had somehow convinced everyone in one of the bars that they couldn't drink anything but Fourex and that they couldn't leave the bar until the beer-can tower he was building hit the roof. He was good at getting people into a game, and it didn't matter what the game was. He was also good at getting people to do things. But what he wasn't good at, on that trip, was picking his women. One night, he and I and a couple of the other boys with us on the trip were in a bar in French Noumea. Dan thought that he was doing extremely well chatting up a couple of very good looking locals. They could speak a little English but he couldn't speak any French. Unfortunately, Dan left the bar with these girls only to find out shortly after that they were in fact transvestites. I can't elaborate on how he found out, because I was with him, but we were gentlemen and quickly left.'

The knowledge that really hard guys don't talk, they act, acquired in the playground at St Laurence's, is why I was never a sledger on the football field. I never wasted time or energy making threats or enlightening rivals about their wife's, sister's or mother's sex life. Why give a bloke the advantage of a warning? You don't say, 'If you do that to me again, I'm going to belt you!' If he deserves some summary punishment, as the Nike ads say, just do it. If a bloke niggled me, say, by standing on my ankle when my leg was hanging out of a ruck, or pulling me back from entering a ruck, anything to hamper and irritate, I'd cop it for a while, thinking, 'OK, your time's coming,' and then I'd pay him back at the appropriate moment. We'd have a beer together after the game, and the incident would be forgotten. The only player who ever refused to shake hands after we had a disagreement in a game is the former NSW and Australian forward Michael Brial, but more about that dust-up in due course.

I gave blokes a gobfull on the field, but never to intimidate them. Apart from anything else, I'm not the quickest bloke with a smart comment. Just get on and play the game has been my creed. Forget about all that peripheral nonsense.

Sledging was once rare in the international game; not so now. One of the instigators of the trend was former All Black skipper Sean Fitzpatrick, who, I hasten to add, was a top player. I've not much time for sledgers, not even those in my own team. A couple of times when teammates mouthed off at the other team I told them, 'Hey, just shut up.'

Generally speaking, I think sledging is a waste of time. Most players are immune to it and are too focused to let mere words put them off their game. I guess it worked more for Fitzpatrick because he was held in such awe, and having this legend mouthing off could unsettle a young up-and-comer.

Maybe it was because I had a point to prove about my size, but as long as I can remember I've always been prepared to do whatever it took on a football field to get over the top of a rival and protect a teammate. My take-no-prisoners play, whether for St Laurence's, Souths, Queensland or Australia, won me a reputation as an intimidating bloke who would do anything on the field and not worry about the consequences, and that was as important a part of my armoury as scrum-maging, rucking and tackling. Opponents knew that and, with a couple of exceptions, took few liberties with me.

One thing I recall from my early footy days at school is breaking my sternum playing in the Under 13s and being hospitalised for two weeks at Royal Children's Hospital. It was here that I found my Achilles heel, one that I struggle with to this day. I could cope with the pain well enough, but not with the emotional side of things. Due to the bed short-age I was placed in the children's burns unit. Throughout the time I was at the hospital, I ate, played and milled around with these other children, some many years younger than I, who had horrific scarring and other injuries. I was so far out of my comfort zone that I couldn't eat. I was traumatised by their injuries. Here was I with something as relatively minor as a fractured sternum, while these children were scarred for life. Yet they were happy and laughing as though nothing had happened to them. I just clammed up and went into a shell. The same thing happened to me years later. For work experience while I was a police cadet I spent two weeks working at the Challinor Centre near Ipswich. The centre looked after seriously mentally and physically disabled people. With me having led such a sheltered life, their plight profoundly affected me, as had the plight of the child burn victims. I didn't know what to do, how to act. Since that time I have always felt extremely uncomfortable around people with these disabilities. I don't know why. Fortunately, part of the community service work rugby representatives take on is to visit a number of similar places and people, and throughout my time in rugby I made sure I volunteered for these assignments – so I could conquer my fear but also to help.

Few who saw me play in my school days would have picked me as a Wallaby-to-be. There were other kids who were flashier, faster, and scored more tries. Kids who were, at that stage, much better players. So how come I made it and they didn't? How come all those superstars we all knew at school and in junior footy never realise their seemingly boundless potential? I believe it all comes down to opportunity and attitude.

Opportunity? Some kids are lucky enough to play in good teams with players they want to emulate and against top sides they have to bust a gut to beat. They have good coaches who have their welfare at heart, who work on their skills and teach them to be good men as well as good football players. They have supportive parents who happily fork out for the boots and the jerseys, and encourage them whether they win or lose and who drive them from oval to oval through the winter.

Attitude? These days there are a hundred distractions that get in the way of making a career in football, which is hard and – on a cold July afternoon when a 130-kilogram behemoth is grinding your head into the mud of some suburban park where less than a dozen spectators are huddling from the rain – can be bloody painful. Girls, holidays with mates, careers, delicious food, and the demon grog all conspire against playing footy at an elite level. Some kids are the gun standoff at school – everyone's hero, chicks hanging off him, winner of dozens of best and fairest player trophies – then they leave school and play third grade, if that. Who'd blame kids like these for seeking greener pastures. Blokes like me wouldn't blame them, I guess. I can only speak for myself, but I know that the characteristic that separates every Wallaby from all those who never realised their early potential is a desire to win and to do your best at the highest level.

I can't say I ever actually enjoyed playing rugby. 'Enjoy' is not the right word. Packing down against the All Blacks, England or the Springboks is too brutal and just too bloody hard to be classified as fun. How often do you see a Test prop running to a scrum with a smile on his face? It's different for backs. Andrew Slack once told me that he really loved being out there in a game. And I've seen fellows slapping each other on the back and giggling during a match. Me? No way. Eighty minutes of violent physical conflict is just too gruelling. I've seen the guys who run 30 metres to hug team-mates when they've scored a try. I'd hug them in the shed after the game. I never ran an extra 30 metres to hug anyone, because I was tired. I just walked back to halfway, composed myself, locked my mind back on the game, got my heart rate down and made sure I was ready to go again.

But by God, I loved *having* played, having done my job and done it well. Winning was important, but if in my soul I believed I had played as well as I was able, I'd be satisfied. And there was the camaraderie. My respect and admiration for my opponents was boundless, *after* a game. Anyone who plays a contact sport as demanding as rugby is a special bloke, no matter whether he comes from Perpignan, Pontypool or Pago Pago. To me, part of rugby's appeal is having a beer in the sheds with a bloke who, just 10 minutes earlier, I'd been doing my level best to smash.

Someone else I've wanted to smash at various times of our lives has been my brother Martin. Try to figure this one out, because I can't. Three brothers grow up together in a loving home with parents prepared to make any sacrifice for their education and happiness, and two, Michael and me, grow up OK, and the third, Martin, makes a mess of his life. Martin's life went sour because of drugs. A character flaw, just a bunch of circumstances coming together, a bad decision or two, saying yes when no would have been a better option, having the genetic makeup that predisposes you to addiction? You tell me. Mum and Dad were the best parents in the world, but Martin has led a disastrous life. When Martin screwed up, I'd say to them, 'Leave him be. Don't blame yourselves, there's nothing you can do, he's got to pull his

23

own weight and be responsible for his actions.' And they'd say, 'But he's our *son* . . .' It was easy, I suppose, for me to be critical of their attitude to Martin. I'm pretty sure if any of my children ever get into trouble I'll act just the same way.

For all his faults, my brother Martin is a lovely bloke, one of the nicest fellows you'd meet . . . but. For whatever reason, he has something amiss in his make-up: if someone sticks their hand in a fire, then Martin will stick both hands in, then his head as well.

I don't accept his accident made his life turn out the way it has. When he was 18 he was sitting blind drunk outside a Brisbane hotel when he got run over by *two* stolen cars. The guys driving were the ones who had stolen the cars and were being chased by the police. They lost control, mounted the kerb outside the hotel, hit Martin and dragged him along the road. He suffered a broken back and pelvis and numerous other injuries. Today people say, 'Well, he would have turned out differently if it hadn't been for his accident,' but I don't think so. The offenders went to court and to jail, and were out before Martin was out of hospital.

When he recovered he was all right for a while. Despite the horrific injuries he sustained, he worked hard, went to night school, got his builder's licence and started his own building business. He was a very good builder and did a roaring trade. He was married and owned a car and a house. Life was looking up for Martin.

He had always dabbled in the drug scene since he was young without getting involved in anything too serious. But now slowly over a period he started to slide into more sordid habits. Little by little Martin's life spiralled downhill. I knew, and my brother Michael knew, that Martin was becoming a drug addict. I would confront him but didn't expect to get told the truth, so I let it be. Slowly I stopped going around to his house as he would have people over who I did not want to mix with, and we moved further and further apart. I knew he was getting worse but there was nothing I could do. Martin's choice of drug was speed, methamphetamine. Luckily, in one sense, Martin knew how to make methamphetamine so he didn't have to try to get money to buy it. But his ability to manufacture it lit a flame that attracted many drug-addicted moths.

I believe if you want to be a decent and successful person you associate with decent and successful people. The opposite is also true. Martin had the same opportunities Michael and I'd enjoyed, was given every opportunity to succeed, but he made wrong choices. Making matters even worse, was that the drugs contributed to Martin contracting bipolar disorder, a psychiatric disease involving mood swings of mania and depression. The mania is characterised by elation, fast-moving ideas, little need for sleep, and grandiose thoughts and behaviour; the depression by periods when he would not want to talk to people for days.

When Martin was injured he received a good payout. Mum was smart enough to say, 'Mart, you're not having that money. I'm taking care of it for you.' She gave some of Martin's payout cash to Michael and some to me and told us to invest it and pay him back with interest. We did, and that's how he bought his house, and set up his business, which he subsequently lost because of drugs.

My brother today, at 43, has gone through hard times. He has no money and minimal possessions. From a burgeoning building business and life on the up to losing everything took just two years.

There are signs, though, that Martin is starting to emerge from the mire, and he's getting on top of his bipolar disorder. He's started back at work and has again started to feel a real pride in what he is doing. He's the cause of a lot of emotion in our family, old Mart, but we will always love him because he is our brother and son. That's the point about drugs: they harm the body and soul of not only the person taking them, but their loved ones as well.

2

ROOKIE COP

I LEFT ST LAURENCE'S in grade 12 in 1982 with average results. They were better than I deserved because our school received an assisted grading, which bumped up my marks.

From about grade nine I'd wanted to be a policeman. I was one of those kids who likes getting into things all the time, being active and pushing themselves. I thought I could do that in the police force. Although it is now called the police service I still refer to it as a force.

It amazes me every day how the lives of the silent majority are ruled by the noisy, outspoken minority. The changing of 'force' to 'service' was just another one of those examples. In this politically correct world, a deluded few believe that changing 'force' to 'service' will make police more tolerant. Yes, the police are there to 'Serve and Protect' but unfortunately they, on many an occasion, are required to use 'force' to do it. Of course, it would be a wonderful world if force wasn't required, but it is, especially today when personal responsibility is an increasingly rare commodity.

My brother Michael signed up with the Queensland Police in 1975 at age 17 as a cadet straight from school, joining others already two years down the indoctrination path. In the pre-Fitzgerald Inquiry corruption hearing years, people joined the police for life and it became their life – from the young constable, raw and full of enthusiasm, to the old sergeant who had seen it all and was counting down the shirts he had hung in the closet until retirement. They saw themselves making a difference, working to 'Serve and Protect' the community.

One thing I observed as a youngster, from the time Michael joined the police to the time I followed his lead, was this indoctrination process. It wasn't written down anywhere, it wasn't spoken about, nor outwardly acknowledged, but once you joined the police, you were totally consumed by the police life. You worked with police, you socialised with police, you talked police. For many, their previous lives seemed to fade away.

Shortly after his induction, Michael was transferred to far western Queensland, around Charleville, Cunnamulla and Thargomindah police stations. On my school holidays, around the ages of 14 and 15, I would go and spend my time with Michael at Thargomindah, 1022 kilometres due west of Brisbane. To get there, my parents trusted me to make the 16-hour train trip to Cunnamulla, where I'd meet Michael in the police four-wheel drive for a three-hour journey across predominantly dirt road to his patch of the world. It was never a lonely train trip. There was usually a carriage or two of country school boarders making the pilgrimage to their desolate outback home.

Like with rugby, it was camaraderie that drew me to the police. It would take four or so days for Michael to travel by four-wheel drive across the heavy red bull-dust tracks to cover his police beat. It wasn't unusual for him to drive a few kilometres up the driveways of properties to a homestead where he'd be met on the verandah by the occupant. They'd exchange a quick hello and the bloke would assure Michael that all was OK. Then off Michael would go to the next property. He wouldn't stop until the end of the day, often finishing up with a beer and dinner offered by the country folk desperate for human interaction. Michael knew if he stopped for one person's hospitality, he would have to stop for all. Just as well, too, for upon his return to his small quarters attached to the side of the police station, he would inevitably find that members of the stock squad had cleaned him out of beer and stew and left a note stating that next time Michael was in Cunnamulla it was their shout. It was this type of mateship that somehow attracted me.

At that stage of my life, I had only two ambitions: to play rugby union and, because back in the good old days before professionalism, players – even the elite players – had to have a job to survive, be a policeman. So when I left St Laurence's I, like my brother before me, joined the police and spent time at the Police Academy in Brisbane.

Even as a kid I had fairly firm views on law and order, and nothing much has happened between then and now to make me revise them too much. As a teenager, you know right from wrong, what is acceptable and what is not. I dislike people who break the law. I'm not talking about the person who is caught doing 72 in a 60-kilometre zone – they are just statistical fodder; I'm talking about people who assault others, who steal, rape, deal drugs, prey on kids. I have dealt with them all in one way or another. What amazes me, what disturbs and annoys me, are the excuses that a vast majority of them have for perpetrating the crimes. Things like: he's from a broken home; her mother works and is never there to supervise; he was abused as a child. Although many of these explanations are sad in themselves, it perpetuates the problem generation after generation. I have been to homes where the grandfather, father and his 16-year-old son sit on the same couch, while we search for and find drugs. Not *one* of the males in the family has ever had a job. Gone in many quarters is the notion of an honest day's pay for an honest day's work and just plain simple Personal Responsibility. I guess you can sum up my point of view this way: You do the crime, you do the time.

And I mean *real* time.

The judiciary and the corrective services system is not as effective as it could be, and the main reason is that it's run by public servants, rather than people with relevant experience who know what they're doing. The government of whatever persuasion only look for solutions within their political term. The noisy minority of the politically correct are always bowed down to at the expense of the silent majority. They should be told in no uncertain terms to pull their heads in. I agree the judiciary should be given latitude in sentencing so that an offence can have a minimum and maximum period. But the responsibility of parole periods should be left to the corrective services parole board or another such body and tied directly to the attitude and the work done since incarceration.

I believe if someone is convicted of murder or drug trafficking (and I mean real trafficking, not day-to-day dealing) beyond a shadow of a doubt, then they should receive the maximum sentence. A mandatory 50 years of hard labour. That's basically a life sentence. They can work on prison farms, dig water channels, build roads and bridges, and if there's nothing constructive for them to do, they can dig holes and fill them in again. The prisoners can learn hands-on skills so when, or if, they do get released they can be an asset to society and not a liability. Just make them work hard like every other decent person in society does, make them toil for five and a half days a week, 8 hours a day. Then they won't have the energy or time to think about causing more trouble or trying to escape. If they spit in a guard's face or start a fight or get caught with drugs or sodomising another prisoner, that's an appropriate amount of time added on to their sentence. It won't take long for even the hardened to realise that because of their inappropriate behaviour they just worked the last two months for nothing.

If they don't want to work or be a useful member of jail society then they should be treated accordingly. They should be fed well, treated with dignity, given books to read and the minimum required time for exercise. But that is it. They are then locked in a cell. No televisions, PlayStations, educational classes, or other comforts. They are in prison, for goodness' sake. If they do mind their Ps and Qs, toil hard, and are a model prisoner then they can be rewarded by having time taken off their sentence. It's simple: a day of work for a day off your sentence. Every prisoner can understand that concept. The prison experience should make an inmate, when he's finally released, say, 'There's no way on Earth I'm going back in there.'

Just like at school, my academic work at the Police Academy, where I was paid a basic constable's wage of $20,000 per year, was only good enough to pass. But the physical side of my training presented no problems. The Head PE instructor was Wayne Bennett, who became the stalwart Brisbane Broncos, Queensland, and Australian rugby league coach, and Wayne's second-in-command was Bill Turner. A mountain of a man and self-defence specialist and, luckily, like Wayne, a very nice guy. Wayne was going all out to recruit me to the rugby league ranks, while Bill, being a Scotsman, was trying to persuade me to play union. Talk about a tug o' war. I've often wondered where I might have ended up if Wayne had won the day.

For the first twelve months at the Academy I felt like a prisoner. We were only allowed to leave the premises on Thursday nights between 5.00 pm and midnight and from 5.00 pm Friday until midnight Sunday. It was like boarding school. I hated being so cooped up, and I resented the restrictions on our freedom because, to my mind, they were supposed to be teaching boys to be men but treating us like children. We were not getting the life experience we needed to be policemen. Fortunately, the cadet system as I experienced it no longer exists.

The Police Academy is like any other teaching facility, really, only you learn certain unique things like defensive driving and how to shoot a pistol. But theory is theory, and nothing can teach quite as well as experience.

Of course, all that changed after we'd been there a while and had to go out on what they called station duty, when we'd spend a week or two at a police station, seeing how they do it in the field. My first stint was at Brisbane's Holland Park. I remember the first day turning up and meeting the crew I would travel with for the day. The sergeant was straight out of your old-time movie: tall, with a smoke hanging out of the side of his mouth and the buttons on his shirt busting at the seams under the pressure of a well-formed beer gut. Before he said a word, I knew that if anyone had to be chased that day he was not going to be the one to do it. After exchanging pleasantries, and while walking to the car, the sergeant turned to me and said matter of factly, 'You know what they tell you at that Academy, just forget it. We'll teach ya what the real go is. Now, get in the back and shut up.' For all his bravado, in the end he was a pretty good bloke.

I do recall, though, that it only took a few days for me to get my real taste of what the sergeant meant. Right in the middle of a heat wave, a call came into the station from a nearby apartment block to report that a neighbour hadn't been seen for some days. Upon arrival, my partner and I spoke to the caller and she aired her concern. We both walked the two flights of stairs to this person's apartment. Now, I was young and naive but I knew what the smell of death and decay was, and it was emanating from that unit. Instantly, my heart beat started to rise. I didn't really know how to steel myself for what could be on the other side. For all I knew it could have been anything from a dead cat left behind by the owner to a dismembered body.

I don't really know why, but without expecting to receive a reply we knocked on the door of the apartment. No one had a key so I was elected to break in. After two or three hefty blows, I shoulder-charged the door. It gave way and I found myself engulfed by a mass of blowflies and a stench I will never forget. The smell was one that I was used to from my times with my brother in the country: dead livestock or the remains of a roo shooter's prey. But this was different, it came from a human.

Tentatively, the constable and I began to walk around the unit in search of the smell. It didn't take long to see a body wrapped in a blanket in the hallway. It was that of a Caucasian male. I saw a pair of black and bloated feet protruding from the bottom of the blanket. Slowly, my eyes shifted upwards. For a moment I thought I saw a movement. I *did* see a movement. The blanket was moving but we could tell this wasn't due to human movement. We knew that we had to remove the blanket from the body. We looked at the blanket, looked at each other, then back to the blanket. 'You do it,' we both said at once, then, 'No, *you* do it.' Although my partner was no more than 20 years old himself, he pulled rank. 'You're the cadet, you do it.'

I tried to pull the blanket away, and exposed a writhing sea of maggots feasting on half of the body. The other half was near-liquefied. The acids were eating through the carpet right to the concrete beneath. My colleague ran to the balcony and threw up, while the neighbours gathered around disgusted. As a new recruit, 17 years old and wanting to show no chink in the armour, I chided my partner for not being able to hack it. Inside I was trying my best to stop the waves of nausea rising through my body. The remains of the man, who had died of natural causes, was a hideous sight, but one I couldn't take my eyes off. It's like when you know a terrible scene is about to come on television and you shouldn't look but you do. It disgusts you, but you look again. Unlike television, this was a real body, with a putrid smell and maggots.

Once we'd composed ourselves the undertakers were called. Two of them entered the flat with Vicks VapoRub in their nostrils so they could stand the stench. Upon reviewing the remains they passed a few rude comments and one retreated to his vehicle. He returned with what to me looked like a butcher's meat hook with a wooden handle at one end. Slowly and methodically, they spiked the flesh and dragged the remains into a reinforced plastic zip-up sleeping bag. My natural instinct was to turn away in revulsion from the dreadful scene, but I resisted because I knew I had to learn. That was my first real job; welcome to the world of police, I thought.

There was plenty of hard police work, but nothing quite as gruesome, when I spent another station duty stint, at Coorparoo Police Station. They were a good bunch of blokes there who welcomed me into their midst. They worked hard and they played hard, and they encouraged me to join them in both.

After I'd done my time learning the ropes and graduated from the Police Academy, I was sworn in. It was time for my first official posting.

Was I was in luck! Instead of being sent to some far-flung one- or two-man outback station I was posted to a brand new station and barracks at Noosa, the beautiful resort town on the Sunshine Coast, north of Brisbane. This was the best posting I could have hoped for, and the other graduates, who'd been despatched to places like Bamaga and Mt Isa in North Queensland, were green with envy.

Then, as I've proven myself capable of doing over the years, I screwed up. I went out on the town to celebrate my good fortune, and crashed my car into a stationary vehicle. I was called before the inspector who ran the Academy. 'Crowley,' he said, 'your transfer has been changed. You're not going to Noosa anymore, you're going to Nanango.' I said, 'Excuse me, sir, where's Nanango?' He replied, 'Look it up on a fuckin' map. Now get out of my office.' That's the one thing about the pre-Fitzgerald era and pre-political correctness. If you made a mistake, in most instances you weren't demoted, or sacked, you were transferred to somewhere in the middle of nowhere for an unknown amount of time to serve your penalty. It wasn't a short, sharp reprimand; you had to live with your mistake. It was a good learning tool.

I spent four months in Nanango, a town of around 500 people two hours drive north-west of Brisbane. I spent three months there, had a break and then returned for another month. They say you never get used to seeing death, but I came close at Nanango. I saw far too many corpses for a bloke of 19.

The only source of entertainment at Nanango was the local pub, of which there were three. One had an extended licence so the construction workers doing late shifts at the nearby Turong power site and other projects around the area could quench their thirst at knock-off time.

The workers had barracks, called dongers, about 5 kilometres out of town, where a few thousand of them slept. They would do a day or night's work, go to the pub, then return to their donger to sleep it off before rising again for another shift at the site. There were many, many drunken brawls to put down and I definitely honed my fighting skills in Nanango. Mostly, though, I tried to be the negotiator because, with Nanango being 45 minutes' drive from Kingaroy and a similar distance from Murgon, you had to wait a fair while for backup when things got unruly.

Due to the size of the town, there was no accommodation other than the hotels. With my luck being on a hot streak I found upon arrival that the only place available was in the hotel that had the late licence. When I wasn't working I would hang around the hotel and help out by stopping brawls. It was not as if there was anything else to do. Mostly I worked the 4.00 pm to midnight shift as I was the only single man, and the married men shared the day shifts, which was fine with me. After work I would again walk the 200 metres from the station to the hotel, have a beer or two with the remaining patrons and wait to see if trouble broke out.

One Friday a group of five power site workers had their rostered day off. They went to the hotel and got loaded. They arrived around 11.00 am and were sitting in the public bar. Throughout the morning and early afternoon I chatted to them, as they were all in high spirits with a long weekend to look forward to. I went to work my shift at 4.00 pm and left them to continue drinking. When I returned to the hotel at 6.00 pm to have a quick bite, the blokes were still perched at the bar. I returned to work. I learned later that when night fell, they all drove to Kingaroy, which was the place to go if you felt like playing up at a nightclub.

About 11.00 pm the same night my partner and I were

running low on petrol and had to drive to Kingaroy to fill up. Once you are 500 metres from the centre of town you drive into the pitch-black of the country plains. We were approximately 30 kilometres from town. In the distance of the high beam I could see something on the road and slowed. As I got closer I saw that it was the bonnet of a vehicle. Past the bonnet and spread all around were bits and pieces of the interior of a car.

It was utter carnage. To the side of the road I saw a vehicle parked and a middle-aged lady waving us down frantically. The accident had just happened. What we saw next was horrifying. The occupants of the car were the same fellows I'd been talking to just a couple of hours before in the hotel. They'd been to Kingaroy, got even drunker, and, speeding back to their dongers, the driver missed a turn and rolled the car over an embankment. The driver was dead in his seat. The fellow in the front passenger seat hadn't had his seatbelt on and had been flung 30 metres out of the car into a paddock. It took us some time to find him. I ran to where he lay. There was blood oozing from his mouth and eyes, and I could tell from the way he was lying that he was beyond help. Fumbling in the dark I checked for a pulse and he died there in the paddock.

The three guys crammed in the back seat weren't wearing their belts either, but amazingly they survived. They sat there in shock, weeping and asking, 'Why?' and protesting that they had told the driver to slow down. From the view of the wreckage you could see that they had hit the embankment at well in excess of 100 kilometres per hour and rolled at least a half-dozen times. How more of them weren't killed I'll never know.

The deceased driver was only 21, and had a wife and two

children. My partner and I had to locate the family in the local caravan park where they were living just out of Nanango and tell the woman her husband was dead. This was the first time I'd ever had to carry out this terrible duty. There's no easy way to break such news, so I simply knocked on the caravan door and gave it to her straight. I hoped, with my youth and limited experience as a policeman, I'd be able to handle the aftermath. The screaming, the crying, the raw anger that poured from a young woman whose life has just been destroyed. I stood there. What do you say, how do you comfort someone in the midst of such tragedy? What seemed an eternity was really only minutes before a neighbour arrived, awoken by the wife's wails, allowing me to slither into the background.

Being a rural area, it was the police's job to assist with the removal of bodies and loading them into the transport. The local doctor in Kingaroy had a strange ruling, which was that if there was a death requiring an autopsy it had to be done straight away, morning, noon, or the middle of the night. This was way after midnight, and it was now raining heavily and my partner was still working with the local Traffic Accident Investigation Officer on taking road measurements. So I had to assist the mortician in taking the bodies to the morgue for processing. Following him through the Kingaroy Hospital entry, I could see through my windscreen a good 50 metres to the rear of the old country buildings a small 5- x 7-metre plain orange brick hut with a pitched tiled roof. This was the morgue, the place that does not discriminate according to race, colour or creed, or whether you have been good or bad. The inside was painted plain white. There were a couple of small roller chambers to keep the corpses

39

cold and the room was illuminated by harsh, bright lights. It was our duty to undress the bodies, tag them, and load them into the refrigerated chambers until the doctor arrived. As soon as this was done the mortician left to return home to his interrupted sleep.

On arrival at the morgue I met the doctor, a middle-aged gent. I'd done an autopsy course at the Police Academy, where, with 20 or 30 other cadets in an amphitheatre, a doctor conducted an autopsy like a military operation. It was detached and impersonal. We didn't know anything about the corpse or his history. But here lying in the morgue in Kingaroy were *real* people with real lives and families, people with whom I'd associated and communicated.

Many people do not realise that unless the deceased has seen a doctor recently about the condition that caused their death, an autopsy must be performed. The body is opened up and the major organs such as the liver and the heart are examined so that it can be determined that the obvious cause of death was in fact the real cause of death. The person performing the autopsy then slices around the scalp, pulls the skin of the face down and with a pneumatic saw cuts the top of the skull off so the brain can be taken out and dissected. Because the brain won't fit back in the skull cavity it is put into the belly and the body is sewn back up.

The doctor told me I had to assist him in the autopsy. 'Put on some gloves,' he said. Reluctantly I did as I was told. I'd handled the internal organs of animals before while kangaroo shooting with my brother, but to hold the organs of a person whom only hours before I'd been having a conversation with, whose wife I'd just informed of his death, was something very different.

Just like when they were picking up the pieces of that poor man's body from the carpet, I thought, 'Hell, what am I doing here! This is madness.' It was, but it was also an education.

That wasn't the last autopsy I helped perform while I was stationed at Nanango. There were two more. In one, a little child aged two had drowned in a dam. And then a 12-year-old boy who lived on a local farm had his throat slashed when he crashed his motorbike into a barbed-wire fence in a paddock. His cousin from the city was riding pillion. The cousin was thrown clear and escaped with only minor injuries. Somehow, despite losing blood from his severed jugular vein and the terrible pain, the injured boy managed to walk a kilometre to return home to his mum and dad. He died in his father's arms.

In the case of the drowned child, I had to tell his parents that their son was dead. I have never had a more gut-wrenching experience. To this day the deaths of those two children affect me. I was only 19 then with no kids of my own, so I guess I couldn't really have appreciated their anguish. Now I do have children I realise how bad it must have been for those people. As bad as life gets.

I had to take the bodies of both boys to the morgue and again assist the doctor – the hospital didn't supply a trained assistant – when he did the autopsies. I can't blame the doctor, because to do his job he had to remain desensitised to the process, but he seemed so uncaring when working on the lads' ruined bodies. I tried to tough it out and pretend I was as detached as he was. But inside I was deeply upset.

* * *

In 1985 I was transferred to Gympie. I'd been planning to play my first year of grade rugby, with Souths, that year but Gympie, two hours' drive north of Brisbane, was just too far to commute to play and train. So I made the best of it and played league with a couple of police colleagues for the Gympie Rainbows, and on Saturdays I packed down as a front rower or hooker with the Gympie rugby union side against teams such as Noosa and Nambour in the Sunshine Coast competition. It worked out well, because I made myself many good mates. I was also picked in the Sunshine Coast representative team, and believe I would have been picked for the Queensland Country side if the coach hadn't been a fellow I'd played against, a breakaway for the Sunshine Coast, who – how can I say it – wasn't exactly a fan of mine. This bloke and I rubbed each other up the wrong way and we had a number of fights on the field. He never got the better of me out on the paddock but he made sure he did in the selection room.

It was at Gympie, when I was 19, that I met a gorgeous girl. She was 16. Her sister was going out with a teammate, and I plucked up the courage to ask her out. She's still putting up with me – and our four kids – today.

After Gympie, I was transferred to the Woolloongabba police station in South Brisbane. I was getting on in the force. I had racked up only 12 months' service but I enjoyed working hard. And if you're a police officer, working hard means arresting people, because there's a never-ending supply of people breaking the law. I didn't wait around to be assigned a job. For a short time I had to ride a police bike, a Yamaha 900, because I'd done the police bike course, and the normal rider was on holidays. I would keep getting into trouble from the traffic boss for going to break and enters and other calls for assistance. I wasn't that interested in writing out tickets like a trained monkey. I wanted to get involved with serious offenders who had harmed other people. Armed robberies were a twice weekly event around that time.

My old schoolfriend Ian Cameron was on the scene then, himself in uniform. 'Once Dan and I were driving near the ramps at the casino near Mary and Elizabeth streets in Brisbane. He said, "Wouldn't it be the best way to die, to get in the car and drive up that ramp at 150 kilometres an hour and just go on and on into the sky?" He worried me sometimes. I thought he had a death wish. Another time, against my better judgment, I got on the back of Dan's motorbike when we were at Mermaid Beach on holidays. Dan rode very, very fast. I said, "Look, promise you won't go over 60 kilometres an hour." Dan did go at 60 kilometres an hour, but only for the first 60 metres, then gunned the bike. I was terrified and put my arm around his throat, yelling, "Stop! Stop!" Dan said to me, "Ian, let me give you some advice: it's not a good idea to be choking the life out of the driver when you're going as fast as we are."' No, some of the things I did as a youngster weren't too smart, but none of us can change the past. Only the future.

One Sunday summer afternoon I was working a 4.00 pm to midnight shift around Brisbane in a marked car with a female partner who, as a senior constable, outranked me. We received a call on the short-wave radio. A monster truck, dual wheels front and back, was being chased by members of the drug squad through South Brisbane, and at the wheel was a ferocious-looking bikie character.

Slowly we meandered across town, not really wanting to get involved, but intending to see if we could assist. As we listened to the call we knew they were heading our way. We stopped our car across one side of the road and another police vehicle stopped across the other to make a road block. The idiot would have to stop or smash into us. I saw the truck round a bend and it was really powering. It came closer and showed no signs of slowing down. It kept coming and coming, and soon we realised the guy at the wheel had no intention of stopping and was prepared to drive right over us. I drove out of his way and he tore past us at 130 kilometres an hour. It was me who was the idiot in thinking that he would actually stop. We took off after him, and soon were joined by other police cars, all blaring their sirens.

The truck was going flat chat. Down the hills it would pick up speed and go even faster, but on the inclines it would slow. The driver refused to stop. We couldn't do a thing but stick with him and hope we could bring the chase to a halt without us, the maniac at the wheel, or a member of the public getting killed. After we'd followed him for about 10 minutes we saw that he was approaching a busy intersection. Would he stop if the light was red, or keep going?

I pulled alongside the truck's cabin, and my partner aimed her gun at the bikie and yelled at him to stop. He laughed at her and flipped her the bird. Straight through the intersection he went, without slowing down. If it had been any day other than a Sunday, someone would have been killed. After the intersection he started trying to ram our car. What was this bastard on? Have you ever seen that film *Duel*? If so, you'll know what we were going through.

At last four squad cars, including our own, managed to hem the truck in, but still the driver wouldn't stop. Not even when one officer fired into his tyres. One tyre blew out, but he had seven more and raced on unhampered, from time to time swerving his truck at the police cars either side and in front of him, which was us. I thought, 'Stuff this bloke,' and decided I'd call his bluff.

I slowed right down, hoping he'd have had enough and would pull up behind us and give up. But I watched in the rear-vision mirror as the bikie lined us up and accelerated. He drove right into the back of our car. Our boot was under his front chassis and he was shunting us along the roadway at 60 kilometres an hour. 'Ohhhh, bloody hell!' was all I could think of to say. After fifty metres of this, we hit a grade and the truck's momentum slowed enough for the other squad cars to block the truck's progress. Officers leapt out, guns drawn. Undeterred, the bikie calmly revved his truck, slammed it into reverse, slid off the rear of our car and piled into the police car behind. One officer standing on the road-way jumped for his life. The bikie shoved the rear car back with his tray going into its windscreen, then threw the truck into first gear and rammed our car again. We were shunted off the road into the footpath.

The truck took off again, with half-a-dozen police shooting at his tyres. Finally he ran out of rubber. His tyres were shredded by bullets. His metal rims were clanking on the bitumen. He climbed out of the cabin. A massive boy, tattoos, leathers.

Full of drugs and alcohol, he was laughing and taunting his captors about how many it took to capture him. He was charged with attempted murder. Of course, we received a pasting from the media and the do-gooders for using our guns. But what would have happened if we hadn't shot his tyres out and that fellow had gunned his truck through a red light? He could have killed a dozen innocent motorists and passengers.

In time, a mate suggested I try to get into the CIB, the Criminal Investigation Branch, but back then entry was based not on your ability but on who you knew and how many years of service you'd notched up, so I missed out.

Then I applied for the Licensing Branch, which would have meant going around to the brothels of Brisbane and saying to the girls working there, 'OK, whose turn is it to be arrested tonight?' and in a couple of days five or so of them would receive a summons in the mail. It was a blessing in disguise when I missed out on the Licensing Branch, too, because it would have been the end of me. The boys also used to drink heavily, and a lot got into serious trouble with the Fitzgerald Inquiry.

Finally, one of my superiors asked me if I'd be interested in being an undercover detective. I said, 'Oh, yeah, I'm up for anything.'

3

SCHOOL OF HARD KNOCKS

MY BANISHMENT TO THE wilderness of small rural police stations was over by 1986, when I was posted to Brisbane. Being back near the action again, I figured it was the right time to see if I could cut it as a first-grade rugby player. Souths, the team I'd played my junior football with when I left school, was my local team, and I had always hoped to play for them before being posted away with the police force. I knew most of the players, so now I made a beeline to Chipsy Wood Oval, named after the Souths stalwart.

Souths' A grade team was a strong one, in spite of their not having won a premiership since 1958, with a number of players who played in state and international games, or would do so in the future, including Wallaby skipper Andrew Slack and the Australian hooker Tom Lawton. It'd be good to be able to say that I made a positive impression on these giants of the game. Unfortunately, I can't. Here's how Tommy Lawton recalls me, circa 1985:

'The first time I met Dan he'd just come down from Gympie. He turned up at Souths training. I think it was my brother Rob who said, "This guy's coming down from Gympie to try out for us and he's a cop." I said, "Oh great, just what we need." Given that we were getting together a crash-hot side then, I thought there was bugger-all chance of a green kid who was very much on the small side making the grade as a prop, which is the position he'd set his heart on. My brother, who played loose-head prop, and I were both Wallabies and so we made up the front row but we were looking for someone with excellent scrummaging skills to take up the tight-head side, which is arguably the most important position in the pack.

'So in walks Dan talking about how he wanted to pack down alongside us in first grade. We all had a look at him . . . and when we stopped laughing because he seemed so very small, we said, "Well, that's great, Dan. But why don't you start in fifth grade and work your way up?" Of course, Dan being a stubborn bastard, he didn't want to hear that at all, and just put his head down and persevered. He was so determined to make it, and in A grade.

'I arranged for the former Wallaby prop Jake Howard, who was my rugby mentor, to come to Souths and have a look at this Crowley kid and tell me what he thought. Jake did so and when he called me back he didn't mince his words. "Mate, there's nothing to him. He's just too small." My thoughts exactly, so we did Dan no favours, and it's a credit to him that he hung in there against the odds and with all of us wanting to give him the flick.

'The first time we packed down together my brother and I had to carry Dan because he hadn't acquired the essential tight-head technique. He was incredibly strong, as strong or stronger than much bigger blokes and way stronger than anyone his own size, but in the front row, technique is incredibly important, things like knowing how to wrestle or manoeuvre your upper body into a position where your opposite prop is pushing against you but actually working against himself.

'But Dan proved us all wrong, I'm happy to say. He had a belligerent, never-say-die attitude to teammates and opponents; he worked very hard and learned the art of scrummaging very quickly, and after a season or two he became a very good technician indeed and an integral part of our team. From then on, we all got along fine. I was just about to finish my career when he was starting, so I'm hoping he learned a bit from me and Rob.

'But having blokes there to tell you what to do is only half the battle. What makes a front rower succeed in this hardest of positions to play is his ability to absorb information and process it and put it into practice. That takes commitment, courage and the ability to stand pain. The skills of rugby are basic and finite. There are certain things to be mastered and in the time-honoured way. Adapting the basics to suit yourself or trying to improve on the tried-and-tested way of carrying them out leads to disaster. There's the right way and the wrong way, just like there's the right and the wrong way to build a skyscraper. Lay the foundations and take it from there. If there were 500 ways of building a skyscraper then every builder would be doing them. There's one way to do it and you do it properly. So, Dan was smart enough to build the correct foundations for being a prop and he prospered.

'It was my privilege to see Dan develop into a craftsman from a raw block of clay, so to speak. He had to compensate for his lack of size. What made him so successful for so long was that few rival props were as skilful as he was. There were occasions where he got pushed around and beaten – purely because he was playing against a bloke with similar skill, and who was bigger.

'Another thing about Crowls is that he never shut up in a game or at training. He'd just talk 'n' talk 'n' talk, forever yapping on about what we should be doing and how we should be doing it. He could pull it off because he never asked anyone to do anything he wouldn't do himself. My fondest memory of Crowls is him out on the field with his finger through his double mouthguard, holding it open while he just incessantly talked. Why did he talk so much? Maybe to calm his nerves. Who knows? Just an idiosyncrasy. All good front rowers are a bit weird.

'Everything had to be in order for Dan. He'd front up to training and say to the coach, "Now, tell me exactly what we're going to be doing today . . . Now, tell me exactly what time we'll be finishing." He had to know and be totally comfortable with it or he wouldn't be happy. There's a bit of the obsessive-compulsive in Dan. He divides his life into little compartments – his footy, his job, his family, his mates – and each compartment has to be under control.'

At St Laurence's I wasn't considered good enough to be chosen in the Queensland schoolboy rugby teams, probably because I didn't attend a GPS school. But even when I was in my late teens and did make the state teams from playing with

Souths' junior sides, I just put my head down and did my best. Not for a moment did I think I was up to top grade senior state standard.

In 1986, as a tyro in the Souths team, I was selected to play for the Australian Under 21s in a tournament that was the curtain-raiser for a Wallabies–Argentina Test at the Sydney Cricket Ground. Taking part in the Under 21s games were such future stars as my old teammate Peter Slattery; Ricky Stuart, who became a dual union/league international and now coaches the Sydney Roosters and the NSW State of Origin league team; and Wallaby winger Paul Carozza.

After our match we were all in the Jacuzzi drinking beer and making a load of noise when Alan Jones, who was then the Wallaby coach and is now an influential and top-rating Sydney radio broadcaster, was trying to give his post-match address to the Wallabies in a nearby room. Jones in his larger-than-life manner stormed to the window and bellowed at us to be quiet. Then one of us, I can't remember who, did the unthinkable to the formidable coach and yelled out, 'Ah, get stuffed!' We all ducked under the water. No one talked to Jones that way. Knowing him, he is probably still tracking down that insolent juvenile. Actually, we had to drag a couple of the boys to the surface before they drowned – that's how scared of Jones they were.

That night, we young blokes went out to a function, and I'm afraid we all got plastered. I don't remember anything about the night, where we went, how we got home. Nor do any of my teammates. Next morning I flew back to Brisbane. Soon after I arrived home I got a call from John Fordham, the manager of the Australian Under 21s, who is today my manager. 'Dan,' he said, 'we've got a couple of problems . . .

51

someone has done a slight bit of damage to a door and a room and also abused a couple of the Argentinean players and behaved badly in the hotel bar. Did you have anything to do with it?' I said, 'No, or not that I recall,' and I was telling the truth. He went on, 'OK, I'll ring the other boys because it's a very serious matter and could affect your footballing future. Whoever was involved should own up now. I'll talk to you later.' Two days later, Fordo called again. I was terrified. What if it *had* been me who'd misbehaved. I could see my rugby career disintegrating before my eyes. I felt guilty as hell. 'Fordo,' I said, 'was it me?' He laughed. 'Dan, it's all sorted. We've finished our investigation and you weren't involved. Thank you for your honesty.' 'Then who was the culprit?' I asked. 'Well,' he said, 'it was actually one of our management.' This was an ex-Wallaby who was not a fan of the Argentineans. Nothing was ever said. You wouldn't get away with it in this day and age.

Another memory I have from that tournament is of Bob McCarthy, the rugby league champion of the '60s and '70s, who was there in some capacity. One of his sons was playing. At a training session before the tournament kicked off, my new boots gave me blisters, which covered my feet and my heels. The sores were killing me, and soon became infected. The doctor had to give me a pain-killing injection in my heel just so I could get onto the field. It didn't work and with 15 minutes to the end of the game and us in front I limped off. That's when Bob McCarthy started bagging me. He said I was weak-gutted and I'd never make it in footy because I couldn't cope with pain and that was the difference between league and union players. He may not even remember the incident today, but I've disliked McCarthy ever since – sometimes it doesn't take much.

It was in the Under 21s that I first crossed paths with Sam Scott-Young, a powerful, incredibly aggressive forward for Souths, Queensland and Australia, who is still a good friend and one I would trust with my life. Seems I made quite an impression on him: 'When I first met Dan he had long hair, a couple of earrings. I thought, "What a lout." Then he explained that he was working in the police force, and had just started in undercover. When I moved from Talba to Brisbane he encouraged me to play for Souths alongside him and Tom Lawton, Garrick Morgan, Tim Horan, Jason Little, Troy Coker – all Wallabies. It was quite a side. There were times, however, when I didn't thank him for smoothing my way into the team. To this day I have all these scars on my face from playing with Crowls because with his short legs he could never step over me when he was piling into rucks and mauls, so he'd step *on* me. I always finished matches with cuts and bruises and most of them were inflicted by Crowley. I'd say to him, "Why are you kicking me? Please stop it, will you? It's the *other* guys who are supposed to kick me!" He'd just laugh and reply, "Sammy, it's better if it's one of us than one of them." That's the kind of relationship we had for many years.'

All through my school footy career I'd never played in a team that won a grand final, so imagine how I felt when in my first season in grade, with Souths' A grade side, we won the Brisbane competition.

I spent the first part of 1986 learning the ropes and being bashed around by the old hard heads. The truth was,

I relished the adversarial aspects of rugby. As Ian Cameron recalls: 'Dan loves to play it hard. At Souths he played a pre-liminary final and a grand final with two broken hands. He endured enormous pain – as he did right throughout his career – but it has to be said that he broke his hands punch-ing someone during the match.'

I took on board the punishment I was dealt, and took note of my rivals' skills too. Back then, a rival prop would give you a pasting on the field and then later in the bar he'd pull you aside and, over a few beers, he'd say, 'Sit down, young fella, here's how I reckon you can improve your game . . . Remember in the scrum you did such-and-such; well, I reckon if you'd done so-and-so, you would have got me.' Or, 'If you'd dropped your shoulder on me you would've had your shoulder on the top of my neck and I'd have been rooted. But you let me get underneath you.' Blokes like Cameron Lillicrap and Andy McIntyre, Wallabies who played in the front row for the University club, were just so generous to younger players like me, when no one would have blamed them if they'd not wanted to help out a fellow who might be challenging for their Queensland and state spot one day. Unfortunately, in this day and age, the top-line guys are flat out all season playing Tests and Super 12s, and they simply don't get to play very many club matches at all, and consequently don't get to pass on their knowledge to young up-and-comers.

Right through my long career, I always tried to follow my own mentors' example by helping young props, like Tommy Lawton, Cameron Lillicrap and Andy McIntyre helped me, regardless of whether the kid was a threat to my position. Says Tom: 'When Dan was playing first grade at Souths, he put a lot of work into the young blokes in the lower grades. A lot of guys won't do that. They feel threatened by up-and-comers who might take their spot. Dan was confident in himself and in his ability to hang onto his position in the team. And the great thing about it also is that he played enough rugby in the "old" days, the days before professionalism, to understand that rugby's a great game for people from every walk of life. It's a great leveller. You can be the king or the dunce. You can be tall or fat. Fast or slow. He reinforced that. Dan had a lot to give in terms of advice, but the biggest contribution he made at Souths was his enthusiasm. He was optimistic and positive about outcomes. Elite sportsmen need to have that expectation of victory, and Dan certainly had that.'

No one really expected Souths to be premiers. Yes, we had an excellent coach in Gary Bird, some fine players in Slack, Tom and Rob Lawton, Anthony Knox and the slippery half-back Stephen Tait. Putting pressure on the top-grade centres was a 17-year-old rookie inside centre who was skilful, slick and speedy and looked like he might go places in the game. His name was Jason Little. Our skipper and No. 8 was Englishman Andrew MacFarlane, a strong, hard bloke who inspired us all. But there was a green tinge about that Souths team, too, because there were me and three or four other young blokes in the team. Many fans thought we'd been selected prematurely. To prove these people wrong was deeply satisfying.

Just a couple of years before, Souths were the easybeats of the comp and it was nothing out of the ordinary for the A grade team to be flogged by 70 points. But in '86 it was us who handed out the thrashings.

Gary Bird, who would later lose out to John Connolly for the Queensland coaching job, worked us harder at training than most other union teams of that era. He was a no-frills coach, a methodical man who believed that the ability to graft hard in a game was as much a key to victory as technical excellence. Every training session it was, 'OK, forwards, whether you want to, or whether you don't, you're doing 50 scrums. Now, get on the scrum machine.' We had a break-away named Mickey Carroll, one of those fellows who just can't tell a lie. Gary knew that and put him in charge of our scrummaging while he went off and worked with the backs and then he'd return and ask Mickey how many scrums we'd done. 'Aw come on, Mickey,' we'd whinge, 'let's knock off at 40 and you tell Birdy we've done 50.' We pleaded, we offered bribes, but never once were we able to persuade him to bend the truth. Much to our benefit, and to mine, in the long run to learn early that to succeed you can't take short cuts.

All that year our main rival for the title was the all-star Brothers team. They were a crack outfit whose playing roster included Wallabies Peter Grigg, Rod McCall, Damien Frawley and Mark McBain. Brothers had dominated the Brisbane competition for the past decade and had handed Souths some pretty substantial beatings in the recent past. When I played with Souths Colts as a kid I remember wincing as Brothers thrashed our A grade side on a pretty regular basis. To many rugby pundits our chance of defeating them in the grand final was a long shot, but we were confident that if we played to our potential we could do the job.

One bloke keener than most of us to prove a point to Brothers and particularly to his rival hooker, Mark McBain, was Tom Lawton. These two warriors had a fierce rivalry and had played against each other for a number of years. Mark was usually picked for Queensland, but Tom was preferred for the Australian team. I could only imagine how Mark felt, year in and year out, determined to play for Australia but continually being overlooked by a guy who couldn't beat him for the state spot. Tom felt just as strongly. He wanted badly to play for Queensland and believed that as the Australian hooker he should have raked for his state. The result was that every time they packed down against each other it was a personal duel to out-do the other, a duel within the duel of winning the scrum, and within the duel of winning the game. The prize for Tom was a green-and-gold jersey. For Mark it was a maroon one. I observed at closehand how the intensity rose tenfold in any scrum when these two went head-to-head. (Complicating matters was the fact I was friends with Mark, and if I talked about him in complimentary terms anywhere around Tom at that time he'd have a go at me. I'd get the same reaction from Mark should I mention Tom.) Each guy's mission was to grind the other out of contention, and leave the coach and selectors in no doubt who was the better man most deserving of the coveted jersey. That was definitely the case in the grand final. Who was to know it would take a decade before they came together with a common cause, when a young upstart named Phil Kearns arrived on the Test scene. It was the first time I heard them have a civil conversation.

Sunday, 5 October 1986 was a great day to be a Souths man. In beating Brothers 31–13 at Ballymore we put behind us all those hidings at the hands of the Brethren, all those lean years – 28 of them – without a title. Andrew Slack, hobbling with a corked thigh and a bruised calf muscle, was magical, touching down after an intercept and being instrumental in two of our tries and steadying our backline when they had the shakes in the opening exchanges.

Andrew's brilliant game was one of the form reversals of all time. In one of our semi-finals we played Norths, whom everyone expected us to flog by 60. Everyone except them, and they beat us by that margin. We definitely had taken our foot off the accelerator because we knew our final berth was secure, but even so, Slacky had a shocker, and they scored three of their tries after intercepting his passes. You know you have had a bad game when you win the opposition's Man of the Match award. That unexpected thrashing knocked any complacency right out of us and we went into the grand final totally focused. That thrashing at the hands of Norths was the occasion of one of the most bizarre things I've ever seen in a football game. With five minutes left on the clock we were trailing by 50 points. We were on the attack and the ball shot out along our backline to our centre Tim Gearin. We had an overlap. Tim pivoted, steadied himself and kicked a field goal! Everyone – the referee, the opposition, his astonished teammates – all stopped and looked at Gearin, shaking their heads. That was Tim Gearin. What can I say . . . he's a back.

We forwards – MacFarlane, Carroll, Ken Wills, Vince Keating, Doug Cooper, Alex Harries, the Lawtons and me – also played our part in the grand-final victory. As rugby writer Wayne Smith reported in Brisbane's *Courier-Mail*:

[Souths'] was a disciplined, technically superior perform-
ance which began, as rugby successes invariably do, up
front. Souths' pack took Brothers apart. They toyed with

*them in the scrum, trounced them in the ruck and maul
. . . A special salute must be paid to three scarcely noticed
other than by their immediate opposition. The front row
of Rob and Tom Lawton and Dan Crowley took complete
charge of the scrum . . . [creating] a demoralisation felt
well beyond the confines of the scrum.*

The final whistle signalled some amazing scenes. I've never seen a celebration like it, as euphoric supporters swamped the equally euphoric players. The crowd back at our club filled the clubhouse and spilled onto the playing field. Cheering, yelling, handstanding, weeping people. They came from everywhere to join in the triumph. It was a great night for the club and also for the local area. Rarely in all the years since have I ever seen a Chipsy Wood crowd that came close to the size of that throng, even though we've won many grand finals since. It's the Australian way, I suppose, to take success for granted, and little by little the excitement of 1986 has dwindled, even though our core is as strong as ever. (The only crowd, I believe, to rival the 1986 one, gathered at Chipsy Wood Oval last year, 2004, to pay tribute to Damien Drew, the Souths tight-head prop who had passed away. He was just 30 years old and only recently married. Damien was at pre-season training on Stradbroke Island and he just dropped and died. He had represented Queensland and, in 2001, he had been in the running to earn a Super 12 contract but he snapped his Achilles tendon during a Queensland development tour to Argentina. His death devastated the club not only because it happened at a time when all the guys were around, but because Drewy was one of the most-beloved blokes ever to grace the field in a Souths jersey – everyone who'd ever had anything to do with him turned up to show their respect.)

That night after our '86 grand-final win, we were congratulated by generations of Souths players. Blokes like Tiny Betts, who'd played for Australia and was a life member at Souths, were still part of the fabric of the club, living, breathing and eating it. It was a great feeling to be able to make these special people so happy. With every sporting club, whether it be rugby union, league, cricket, soccer, basketball or whatever, there is a group of people who give of themselves selflessly. These people in both official and unofficial positions are deeply and passionately devoted to the club through the good times and the bad. They are always there helping others succeed by doing whatever it takes. Without them, success is virtually impossible. At Souths we were blessed with many of these. Our grand-final win meant as much to them as it did to the players.

Today, Rod McCall is a good friend. Back then, as a Brothers' second rower, he was my natural adversary in the willing games we had against each other. Rod still insists on telling this tale against me: 'When he was a motorcycle cop, Souths played my team, Brothers. There was tremendous rivalry. In the mid-'80s they played two grand finals. We won one, they won the other. One day, Dan turned up late for the match, as he's wont to do. He'd been at work. He roared in on his motorbike, wearing his uniform, 20 minutes before kick-off, through the gate at Brothers' ground that they keep open for officials only, and parked his bike right near the goal posts. Dan dismounted and hustled off with his kit bag to get changed. Next time I saw him the game was in full swing.

It was a top match, with many Wallabies on the field. Throughout, Dan was really giving it to one of our forwards. I thought I'd better put a stop to that so I reached through from the second row and gave Dan a facial, just slapped him around a bit. Problem was, one of my fingers jabbed him in the eye. He blew up. "Right!" he yelled, "Which one of you is gouging? If I find out who you are, I'll kill you." I didn't own up. For the next decade or more Dan would never shut up about Brothers having been filthy gouging bastards and if he ever found out who gouged him in that scrum . . . One day we were in the clubhouse throwing rums back together and I decided this had gone on long enough. "Crowls, I have to confess . . . *I* was the culprit, but I didn't mean to gouge you." He yelled, "So it *was* you, you bastard! I always suspected that!" Other than the fact he holds a grudge, Dan's a good bloke.'

It was a wonderful feeling to win that 1986 grand final and we all enjoyed the moment. Yet, it's funny. It wasn't until we lost in '87 that we realised just how sweet our victory had been. That first year in grade was an education for me. It was playing with the Lawtons that taught me what I had to be able to do on the field and in the scrum if I was ever going to make it as a good prop. But, as Tommy says, knowing what to do and actually doing it are two very different things. So I worked hard at my trade, I studied teammates and rivals and learned what separated the good scrummagers from the so-so ones. I kept discovering new aspects of scrummaging until the day I stopped playing. Looking back, my scrummaging technique was probably my most valuable asset and the main reason I played in 39 Tests over 10 years, made three

Australian World Cup squads, appeared in 125 games for Queensland and 165 first-grade games for Souths.

At school, because of my size, my coaches were always trying to talk me into playing hooker. I did play there a bit in grades 10, 11 and 12, but my specialty position was tight-head prop, the position played by the strong, nuggety blokes with limited speed and ball skills. Who knows, maybe I'd have had a more successful career had I been a hooker. Too late to worry about that now.

The teachers at St Laurence's were the first, but not the last, to tell me I was too small to play prop. Alec Evans, as I've already mentioned, was one who popped up continually throughout my career with the same comment, even though I know he appreciated my aggressive nature, which enabled me to go out on the field and dig in and stick it out. In many ways this excellent rugby technician was a great help to me. I guess he felt that if I was going to hang around he'd help me be the best that I could be. Even Topo Rodriguez, the Argentinean who was a mighty prop for New South Wales and the Wallabies for some years, had a cryptic shot at me. Mixing his imperial and metric measurements, he said that as far as he was concerned, a prop 'had to be three figures both ways, that is, 5 foot 10 or taller and 100 kilograms or heavier'. At 5 foot 9 and about 98 kilograms – my usual playing weight in those years – I was neither. Then, again, I took Topo's words with a very large grain of salt. Although he was Argentinean, he was, after all, playing for New South Wales, so I'd expect nothing less of him.

I first came across Alec Evans when I was playing school-boy rugby in grades 11 and 12. He was the coaching master at Brisbane Grammar School, and was also the state schoolboys' coach, and he went on to coach the Reds, and be assistant to Alan Jones on Jones's Wallabies 1984 Grand Slam tour, so he's always been a major player in Queensland rugby and a bad man to have pitted against you. He had a belief that props must be huge, and that a good big prop will always beat a good small prop. He's probably correct in a general sense, but I was unwilling to move from a position I'd always enjoyed playing, and knew I could out-do my opponents at the highest level with a technique that owed more to skill than size and brute power.

I figured out early that my only chance of making it as a top-class tight-head prop was to hone my scrummaging technique. My aim was to be a better scrummager than any fellow I packed down against, so my wiles could compensate for my relative smallness. The combination of my natural strength, chronically cranky disposition and ever-improving technique was what got me selected in Souths' front row in 1986, and made Tommy Lawton revise his early negative opinion of me.

Playing prop is a learned skill. Some backs were born fast or elusive or with natural ball skills; lineout jumpers are usually helped by their tall genes; but no one is born knowing how to play prop. It's something you pick up as you go along, by playing with and against the best. I have never backed down from a quote I gave a reporter some years ago: 'I reckon the only way you can learn to be a good prop is to have your head shoved up your arse a thousand times, and the *really* good props are the ones who never get their head shoved up there the same way twice.' The more scrums you pack the more you learn. The more times you get beaten, the more times you learn how not to get beaten that way a second time. It's also about being able to reach a level of intensity where you're not going to be overcome; you're not going to lose. As Tom Lawton instilled in me: 'You can lose the game, but if a prop overcomes his opposite number he's still entitled to feel satisfied.'

Tight-head prop is an extremely hard position to play. You are the anchor of the scrum and must be able to bear enormous pressure and inflict it on your opposite number. If you can dislodge the tight-head prop, you can dismantle his scrum. You are the cornerstone. Former Wallaby prop Jake Howard always maintained that the most important bloke in any Test team was the tight-head prop and the second most important bloke was the reserve tight-head prop.

If you're playing tight head, you've got two guys – the loose head and the hooker – boring down on both sides of you so you have to pack at exactly the right angle; first, to avoid being snapped in two, and, second, to anchor your scrum. A good hooker beside you can make life a lot easier by soaking up the pressure. I was lucky when I first started at Souths because in Tom Lawton I had a 120-kilogram gorilla as my hooker and he took a lot of pressure off me. He knew what he was doing.

However, it wasn't until Tom played tight head himself that he realised what we tight-head props go through every scrum. He packed down in the position once in a reserve-grade game and I can remember him laughing before the match when he saw the player he'd be opposing. This guy was about 95 kilos tops and Tommy called him a 'Biafran' and licked his lips at the prospect of steamrolling him all over the scrum. Well, it turned out that the Biafran was a seasoned tight head and it was the much bigger Tommy who was steamrolled. He got such a workover he couldn't get out of bed the next day. He said, 'Bugger playing tight head for a joke,' and never ventured there again. Hookers have a whole different set of skills to master, and Tommy had a newfound respect for the skills, technique, strength and stamina a tight-head prop needs just to survive.

Life for a loose-head prop is not exactly a picnic but because he has to contend only with the tight-head prop he doesn't have to withstand and exert the pressure that a tight-head front rower does. A loose head is expected to have extra energy to motor around the field a bit, tackling and running with the ball. Fair enough, too.

A strong neck and shoulders is essential for a tight-head prop. As I said, if you can dislodge the tight head, you can dismantle his scrum. But I never worked especially hard building my strength. It was quite enough to train and play over a long period of time. The gruelling nature of the position, with all the requisite pushing and shoving and taking hits gives you all the strengthening you need. It takes a while. When I first started in grade I wasn't used to the tremendous intensity and the morning after a match I literally couldn't get out of bed. Imagine waking on a Monday morning to go to work. You've had a late night and few beers. You've played a game of intense physical activity which is making you ache all over. Then you try to raise your head from the pillow and you can't do it. You try again, but your neck is just so sore, sending shooting pains down your back and into your shoulders. You then shift your body and roll your head across the pillow till you're face down and then roll off the bed or try to stand up from there.

Stuck in a scrum you can't always see what's going on, so you have to be able to *feel* it. If your opponent moves a certain way, changes his stance or changes the direction of the pressure he's putting on you, you have to be able to react immediately and counter him. It's all about feeling what is the correct thing to do. In response, I might put my shoulder down at a little bit of an angle and straighten up my other side, or I might move my left foot up a little bit on the inside which will bring my backside in and enable my second rower to give me more push. After a while it becomes instinctive.

Another thing a prop learns early is that the initial hit – that mighty collision when the two forward packs collide before the halfback puts the ball in and is always accompanied by a huge grunt that can be heard all over the ground – is crucial to the winning of the scrum. It's not about charging in from a distance, but, like those knockout punches a good boxer throws that you never see, short (travelling no more than a few centimetres), swift, immensely powerful, and decisive. (Unlike the ridiculous flailing around that usually takes place when footy players brawl on the field and no one ever gets hurt.) The bloke who has been hit with a perfectly timed short punch goes down for the count and you say, 'How the hell did that happen?' Like that kind of punch, the hit in a scrum is all about timing and momentum.

The trick is to know when the opposing pack is going to come at you, and, with all eight of you driving hard in unison, hitting them a split second before they hit you. You've got to sense and hit.

Packing a scrum and getting your rhythm right is like a rowing race. If you have eight people rowing perfectly in unison, they don't have to row as hard. If they're not all rowing as one they'll be ineffective. It's the same with the scrum. If you've got only six or seven guys hitting and not eight, you're history. If, say, you're playing prop and your second rower pushes late while the opposition have got their hit together, you're going to run into a brick wall and then be pushed backward. Your back will be concertinaed and you'll be squashed.

Every member of the pack has to know the preconceived signals. If the prop or hooker drops his knee, or jinks, that might be the sign to ram. And he has to try to cotton on to the other pack's signals in order to short-circuit them. It's psychological warfare in there.

A prop will be 'popped' – shot straight up out of the scrum – when his second rower is poorly positioned or isn't giving him enough push, or when the opposite prop is a better scrummager or just applying more pressure. (A number of years ago you would try to pop your opposite number; today the manoeuvre is illegal but popping still happens.) When that unfortunate series of events occurs, there's only one way you can go. You're pushed back until you're all hunched up and if you don't pop up you'll be broken in two. Believe me, being popped is a very bad feeling.

The most imposing international forwards I've played against are the South Africans. Against most rugby nations you can play with a slight injury and get by, but against the Springboks there is no place to hide. My first match against them, in 1993, when they'd just been allowed back into the international game, was a nightmare. Queensland had played a match in Fiji on the way over to South Africa, and I'd slipped in the mud and one leg went back and the other forward, and I did this excruciatingly painful lunge in the middle of the scrum. I didn't know it, but I'd suffered a hernia (the tearing of the stomach wall).

I played my first game in South Africa against Natal Province and I lasted two scrums. My hernia was killing me and I had no stomach strength. I tried to cover up that I was hurt but in those scrums, against those huge and aggressive South Africans, there's never anywhere to hide. My opposing prop, Guy Kebble, who was 132 kilos to my 98, smashed me because he was too big and skilled and I was too unfit and too sore to counter him effectively. And there was the fact that he was getting a shove from his 137-kilogram second rower. When we hit as the scrum packed down I tried to angle away from Kebble to evade the pressure he was putting on me, but I couldn't. We collided and he just lifted me off my feet and walked forward. I was about a metre off the ground. I was thinking, 'What am I doing up here?' As the boys said, I didn't need tickets to get to the second tier of the grandstand, I was already there. In the second scrum I tried to move again and I knew I was a goner. I ended up breaking one rib and popping two others and the hernia was killing me. (A popped rib is what you get when the cartilage that holds the ribs in place tears and the ribs are displaced and come out. In some cases they remain displaced. Even today I have number of ribs that stick out from my ribcage. Every time I see them in the mirror I think of Guy Kebble.) I couldn't even lift in the lineout. I said, 'See ya later, fellas, I'm outta here.'

On the bench was Queensland and Australian prop Adrian Skeggs. He was taking photos with a pocket-sized camera of the cheergirls lined up in front of him. I don't know what was funnier, Skeggsy's face when our coach John Connolly told him to put his camera down and get out on the field to replace me, or Connolly's expression when he first saw the awesome Springbok forwards. It was his first experience of them, as well as mine. To Skeggsy's credit and the rest of the team's, he went out there and subdued Kebble, who ran out of wind after four scrums. It was my bad fortune to strike Kebble when he still had some puff.

As a result of that game, John Connolly decided that tight head was no longer my position and shifted me to the open side, figuring that my lack of size would not be such a liability against the good big men coming into the game, and that playing the less-arduous open-side role would leave me with the petrol in my tank to run, tackle and use my ball skills. In shifting me, 'Knuckles' probably prolonged my career by five or six years.

As formidable as Guy Kebble was, the opposing prop who caused me the most grief was the Springbok JJ Styger. He was a pear-shaped, slight-shouldered, unathletic, soft-looking man, yet in his playing days he could get his upper torso down very low and he had a tremendously strong lower back, and he'd shove with incredible power. It didn't matter how low you got, he could go lower, and he kept coming at you and coming at you. It was like packing down against a bulldozer. He only played a handful of internationals. He fractured a disc in his neck and retired. The last time I saw him, he was a dentist and had shrunk from about 125 kilos to 85 and was contesting triathlons.

There's a dark art to playing front row and a number of factors determine how you fare against a rival: whether you're tall or short, have wide shoulders or thin shoulders, whether your technique has been honed playing against large, small, experienced or inexperienced props. Until you actually pack down against a guy you can't know how things are going to turn out. It's not something you can really prepare or train for. If you're a centre or winger, five-eighth, halfback or line-out jumper, you can watch tape after tape and learn your opposite number's idiosyncrasies: whether he steps off his left foot or his right foot, how he fends, how fast he is, whether he chips and chases, when and how high he can jump. The only position on the field where videotape is useless is the front row. Education only comes when you come together in that first scrum, and maybe the second or third. That's when the brain can start ticking over, coming up with ways to counter him, and you have to think fast under pressure before he works *you* out and pulls *you* apart. And just because you get the better of a rival one day, doesn't mean you'll do it again. Because if he's any good he will have changed his technique to one that presents you with more problems next time. It's a never-ending battle.

I wasn't the only international prop who had problems with Styger. But a number of guys had *no* problems with him. It's a funny thing. Olo Brown from New Zealand, who teamed with Sean Fitzpatrick and Craig Dowd to form the All Blacks great front row of the '90s, got the better of most props he opposed but he didn't worry me. And I usually found the New South Welshman Richard Harry, with whom I battled against for a Wallaby jersey later in my career, a handful. Others didn't. It wasn't that he was better than me or I was better than some other bloke. It was just our different physical make-ups and the way we packed and our individual techniques.

Rod McCall had plenty of chances to observe my game when he played against me for Brothers and with me in the Queensland and Australian teams. 'Dan succeeded in a position which is mainly about strength and size by compensating for his size with a tremendous scrummaging technique. His technique was as good as anyone's I've ever seen. He regularly gave away 20 kilos to his opposite number in the most confrontational and difficult position on the field. It takes guts to match it with a bloke who's way bigger than you and is trying to break your body and your spirit and who's fired up and maybe, if he's French or Italian, just had a bottle of red wine to get his juices flowing before the match.'

There is definitely a brotherhood of props. No matter what country we represent, we're the same species. You have to be a bit crazy to do what we do. I reckon props definitely get on better than fellows in other positions. Like, how many wingers do you see hanging out together? Props *understand*. There's a school of thought, too, that we're all so battered and ugly no one but another prop will talk to us.

Prop is the only position in rugby in which you have regular and prolonged physical contact with your opposite number. There's a confrontation in which there is only one object. Get over the top of the other bloke physically and mentally. You're going at it one-on-one all the time. That's your job. If a prop beats his man upfront, it'll usually set the winning platform for the rest of the team. Fail in your duty, and you're out. But for all the ferocity of our battles on the field, I've never known a rival prop I've not wanted to shake hands with and buy a beer after the game.

What else does a good prop need, apart from scrummaging skills, ruthlessness, strength, imperviousness to pain, willingness to put his body on the line, stamina and, these days, excellent attack and defence? Just one thing. As ever, a good attitude. And that means wanting to play and wanting to play *well*, whether it be for his club, state or country. And it means not spitting the dummy when he gets dropped – as, at some stage, he inevitably will – and hanging in there, playing well until the selectors see the error of their ways and reinstate him. I had to wait until Andy McIntyre retired at the end of 1988 to become a regular in the Queensland side, and even though I was a threat to his job Andy helped me no end. Same with me. I knew he stood in the way of my dream to be a Red, but I didn't try to undermine him or psychologically do him over at training (not that it would have worked anyway because Andy was a lot smarter than I was). And Richard Harry, Tony Daly and Ewen McKenzie kept me warming the Wallabies bench on and off from the start of my international career until the end.

By all means if a guy is dropped, he should get annoyed, anyone worth his salt would, but he shouldn't let it manifest itself in a surly or disruptive demeanour that harms the team. On the training paddock and at the game he must switch on and work harder than ever and do whatever he can to help the side, even if that means running the water.

I was in and out of the Australian team right through my career. The reasons? There was a number of good props around, I had my share of injuries, and I had another problem. Maybe I'm being harsh on myself but I feel that I'd go all out to get picked for Australia but when I was in the team, perhaps I relaxed a little, perhaps my intensity flagged, and I would find myself back on the bench. Bob Dwyer once said that if you're No. 1 in your position the only way to stay there is to train like you're No. 2. Maybe sometimes when

I was No. 1 I failed to do that, and that's why I was dropped. Some guys with huge natural ability can get away with not giving 100 per cent in a game or at training, but grafters like me would survive on intensity. I have enormous admiration for fellows such as an Ian Thorpe, Grant Hackett, John Eales and some of our cricketers who make it to the top and stay there for a long time.

And, finally, good attitude means digging in when you're getting bashed and you're losing. I have the greatest respect for an opponent who keeps on coming at me, who keeps going and going and going, never giving up even if he's being shoved all over the park. I learn how good a bloke is when he's going backwards, not when he's going forwards. It's when he's up against it that you learn all about a man's character.

Life is all about character. It doesn't matter whether you are playing elite sport, running your own business, or caring for your family, it's all about how you fight back after setbacks. In rugby, there is a breed of player who keeps bouncing back after a loss to play his best. It doesn't matter if his team has been beaten five times in a row, his intensity or desire to win never slackens. I think of someone like David Wilson, who would keep powering on, no matter what the score or how badly he might be injured. Conversely, there are others whose talent allows them to play at an elite level for a time. Only for a time. Because their inability to handle setbacks like copping a hard knock, getting dropped or beaten inevitably sees them fade from the scene. They haven't the heart or spirit to fight back. Week after week in hand-to-hand combat with the opposition, you quickly get to know which guys are the former, and which are the latter.

4
MAKING IT

IT WAS MY GOOD LUCK to be kicking my grade career off at the outset of a golden age of Queensland rugby. For the first time in ages, there was a bunch of blokes capable of distinguishing themselves in the maroon jersey of our state and winning for Queensland a bigger representation in the Australian side, which had long been dominated by New South Welshmen. I made the bench for Queensland in 1986, and in November when the Queensland Rugby Union, with financial support from Fourex, selected an elite squad who would train together over the off-season and so hit the ground running when the representative games of '87 kicked off, I was in it. I was in good company, too. My fellow squad members included Bill Campbell, Troy Coker, Dave Codey, Michael Cook, Damien Frawley, Roger Gould, Peter Grigg, Anthony Herbert, Rob and Tom Lawton, Cameron Lillicrap, Michael Lynagh, Mark McBain, Rod McCall,

Andy McIntyre, Greg Martin, Jeff Miller, Brendan Nasser, Andrew Slack, Peter Slattery, Brian Smith, David Nucifora, John Mulvihill, Paul Kahl, Sam Scott-Young and Brendan Moon.

In May '87, in my second year in Souths' A grade team, I was selected for Queensland B to play the curtain-raiser to the Queensland–NSW clash at Ballymore. Andy McIntyre, then recognised as the best tight-head prop in the country, bested me for the job in the top side and rightly so. Yet, being picked in the Bs was an indication that my full-on Queensland debut might not be too far away. Bob Templeton was the coach of Queensland then and he was very loyal to the incumbent players, so I knew I just had to bide my time until my opportunity came.

I didn't have to wait long. The next month, with a number of regular Queenslanders playing for Australia in the World Cup that was being staged in Australia at the time, I played my first game for Queensland in a far-from-friendly friendly match against the visiting French club side Languedoc-Roussillon, which sported six Test players.

It was a brutal game from the opening whistle, and it escalated into vicious open warfare in the final 10 minutes. Their breakaway, Philippe Chamayou, had been grabbing our lineout jumpers in the squirrel grip all match long, while ensuring we couldn't return service by wearing a cricket protector. For the uneducated a squirrel grip is where an opponent grabs a player by the testicles, the most vile act in the game after eye gouging. It was one of those matches when, if you put your hand on the ground as the scrum went down there'd be a French boot stomping on it. Gouging, biting, kicking, everything went on. Fights kept breaking out right through the match. I was surprised by their roughhouse tactics, but after the first few minutes I figured, 'OK, that's how the French play,' and got on with my job.

I packed down against the French Test prop Guy Colomine. I recall him running onto the field and he was massive. He had a prematurely old and craggy face, and I thought, 'Bloody hell! I'm going to be packing down against a bloke older than my father. This is going to be a long afternoon!' He dished it out to me, and stamping on my hand was just one of his tricks. I gave him back some, too, but he was the kind of bloke you couldn't hurt with an axe. He also had a very handy backup man in his second-row partner, who every time a scrum packed would release his bind and swing punches through into the faces of our raw front row.

With 15 minutes to go, their centre, Patrick Fort, a Test player, broke his arm, which meant they had to play a man short. We were slightly ahead at that stage, but instead of trying to score points the French decided to belt us, happy to believe that we'd purposely injured Fort. Referee Col Waldron sent off Chamayou, then Colomine for elbowing our second rower, Nigel Holt, in the jaw. Waldron ended the game early, fearing total mayhem – and that he was odds on to get attacked by one of our feral French opponents – after he sent their two off. Those Frenchmen were really going off. A crazy bunch of boys. But that is the French way, I was to find later on in my career. They either come out at you all fire and brimstone or meek and mild, it just depends on how they feel on the day. Unfortunately, opponents of the French never know which way they'll play until the game is underway.

The final score was 24–19, our way. It was my kind of

match, and Sam Scott-Young, another who enjoys rugby when things get willing, and I won praise.

It was great to be picked, even if it was an under-strength Queensland side, and to get my first state jumper. I received my second a few weeks later when my rival and mate Andy McIntyre withdrew with a twisted ankle from a match against the English club side Leicester, at Ballymore.

After the Languedoc-Roussillon game there was an uproar with their president Francis Senegas pleading with the media not to write about those last ugly 10 minutes. Small chance. The media made the match sound like the Battle of the Somme, and they weren't too far off the mark.

Over the years I've been in a bit of strife for my willing approach to rugby. I've had well-publicised confrontations with Michael Brial, Josh Kronfeld, Shaun Hourigan, the Englishman Darren Garforth and others. Rugby is a violent contact sport. Intimidation comes with the territory. All the great forwards have a bit of menace about them, and can instil fear, or at least respect, into an opponent and I suppose I was trying to emulate them.

I heard somewhere that the All Black prop Richard Loe, who is still infamous for opening up Wallaby winger Paul Carozza's face when he tackled him late after Paul had scored a try, would get the upper hand from the outset by grabbing a generous chunk of his rival prop's gut with his huge farmer's mitt in the first scrum of the game and snarling, 'We can do this hard, or we can do it easy. What's it to be?' Richard never tried his claw tactic on me, and I'm happy to report that each time we met we treated each other with great respect, give or take a few rushes of blood. Richard was one of the game's bad boys, but a lovely man off the field. He is one of a breed, including Sam Scott-Young, Justin Harrison, Martin Johnson, Lawrence Dallaglio, perhaps myself and Sean Fitzpatrick, who transformed from friendly, civilised human beings off the field to short-fused enforcers on it. Rugby league has blokes like Adrian Morley and Gorden Tallis who come into that category. I think it's just that we're very competitive and we get fired up, and the adrenalin flows and takes us a little bit far. I've roughed a few blokes up then thought, 'You idiot! You shouldn't have done that.' But in the heat of the moment I'd be doing it again.

No footballer, I believe, wants to hurt an opponent permanently, or to cause serious injury. That can ruin a life, and football is, after all, as I said earlier, only a game. But I don't regard breaking a guy's nose as causing serious injury. Same with rucking. I've had my foot on a rival's head more than a few times, and gone on with it. I regret it. I have no problem rucking the body, but a head is another matter. Still, I'm guilty as sin of having done it, and it's been done to me many times. I got stitched up and there was no lasting damage.

Tom Lawton was with me in front-row trenches for an important phase of my career and, for what it's worth, he offers this insight into my aggressive reputation: 'I know Crowls pretty well and I think even though he would like to have been seen as a tough, uncompromising rugby player I don't think he enjoyed people thinking that he was overly aggressive. There were times when he got into scraps but they were born of frustration more than anything else. He was never one of those players who likes to get onto the field and fight, although he did enjoy being on the edge of violence, which comes with the territory in top-class rugby. It's a violent sport. Still, you need to be able to control yourself if you want to win the game. A penalty, after all, means three points to the opposition, and no team can win if they're a man short.'

Although I mainly warmed the bench again for Queensland through 1988, I played in an early season game against the tough New Zealand side Canterbury. It was my third match for the state. Our scrum was superior, but the backs, in trying to throw the ball around with abandon, gave away too much possession. There was one bizarre moment brought on by the similarities between the Queenslanders' and the Kiwi boys' jerseys. Their skipper, John Buchan, threw the ball by mistake to our Cameron Lillicrap and 'Crapper' got it to our winger, Dean Garnett, who found yours truly backing up for a try. We props don't score too many tries and tend to remember them in great detail, much like a miner recalls finding a gold nugget. I'd got my start in the match because Andy McIntyre had gone on his honeymoon, and as soon as he was available again I was back on the bench.

However, I was hoping that my efforts for the Reds, against the Frenchmen, Leicester and Canterbury, hadn't gone unnoticed, and I'd set myself the challenge of making the Wallaby tour of Italy, England and Scotland at the end of the year.

'It will be with reluctance that the state selectors relegate McIntyre's understudy Dan Crowley to the reserves,' wrote rugby reporter Wayne Smith in Brisbane's *Sunday Mail* after the Canterbury match.

Crowley's coming of age as a representative prop in his [third] match for the state was about the only compensation Queensland can take from its match of squandered opportunities against Canterbury. The 22-year-old Souths front rower had served notice of his promise with a fearless performance in his debut last year against French provincial side Languedoc, possibly the most violent match in which Queensland have played in the last decade. [Against Canterbury] he showed he has the skills to go with his courage.

Hooker Tom Lawton insisted yesterday that there is not a better tight head in Australia, McIntyre included. 'The only thing McIntyre has that Crowley doesn't is experience,' Lawton said. 'Technically there is nothing between them and there is no way Mark Harthill [the NSW tight head] is in Crowley's class.'

Crowley brings talents to the team which not even McIntyre possesses. He is a gifted ball handler by any standards, let alone for a prop, and it is doubtful whether any other front rower could have matched his pace as he loomed in support of winger Dean Garnett and halfback Peter Slattery to score Queensland's third try against Canterbury.

The following month I got my first taste of true international footy when I was selected in a Queensland Country invitational side to take on the visiting English team, which included the great Dean Richards and some handy players in John Bentley, Stuart Barnes and Gareth Chilcott. We were beaten 19–7 in a drab and uninspired match on a windy day and afterwards I told anyone who would listen that I thought Australia would win the Tests. So it proved, with 22–16 and 28–8 wins to the home team. Andy McIntyre and the Lawton brothers formed the Australian front row in the First Test.

I thought I was a good chance to make the Australia B team to play the All Blacks but rising young New South Welshman Ewen McKenzie, today the Waratah's coach, got the nod instead. A sign of things to come.

In another portent, when I played in the curtain-raiser to that game, for Brisbane in a clash against Queensland Country, an Australian selector asked me to have a shot at loose-head prop. Of course, I ended my days in football as a loose head. I was happy to switch because I had my heart set on making the Wallaby tour at year's end and knew versatility would be a factor in my favour.

After I performed well for Queensland B against New Zealand – we got flogged 39–3 but our scrum was immovable and coach John Connolly called me 'the best tight head in Australia' afterwards – I reckoned I had one foot on the plane. And I was further heartened when I was picked on the bench for Australia in the Third Test against the All Blacks at Concord Oval in Sydney. It was a fantastic feeling to wear the Wallaby gold, even if I didn't make it onto the field and even if we got smashed, 30–9, by a great All Black side which included John Kirwan, Joe Stanley, Grant Fox, Buck Shelford, the Whetton brothers, Sean Fitzpatrick and the enforcer, Richard Loe. A fellow reserve was Michael Lynagh, who'd been dropped for the game, so I figured I was in exalted company. Michael had been replaced as five-eighth by Lloyd Walker, who hailed from the Randwick club in Sydney and who was a favourite of the coach Bob Dwyer, also a guy with Randwick affiliations. Lloyd was a skilful player but unfit. Fact was, he couldn't run out of sight on a dark night.

* * *

For many, many years, NSW controlled the Australian team selection. Players such as Lloyd Walker were inexplicably preferred to better-performed Queenslanders, like Michael Lynagh. Parramatta prop Peter Kay, who played just one Test in his life, was chosen ahead of Rob Lawton in the '88 series against England. A number of the New South Welshmen were convinced they were better than us and refused to take us seriously, just because they came from south of the border. Of course, the Blues' attitude rankled with us and this is what triggered many fiery interstate clashes. I'm glad to say that over the next decade I played a part in many Queensland victories.

Being reserve for Australia gave me even more reason to believe that I would be on the plane to Europe for the Wallaby tour at the end of 1988. Then, 48 hours before the team was to be named I received a call from Tommy Lawton. 'Crowls,' he said, 'I've just been talking to Bob Templeton, and, mate, you're in!' Tom and I are very good mates and he was just so pleased to be the one to break the good news to me. Against all my better instincts – I'm at heart a cautious and conservative guy – I rang Mum and Dad and told them I'd been picked for the Wallaby tour and they went straight out to spend their hard-earned money on plane fares so they could see me play. I was beside myself with joy and the inner satisfaction you get when the one goal you've been working toward is within your grasp. I knew that once I got on that trip I could prove to the selectors that I was worthy of playing for Australia.

It's amazing how fast you can go from the heights to the depths. It transpired that Tempo had spoken prematurely and I *hadn't* been picked. I'd been passed over for Ewen

McKenzie. I was absolutely devastated. And so was Tommy, when he realised he'd given me the wrong information. The hardest thing of all was telling my parents to cancel their bookings. Not far behind was missing out on an honour I had strived so hard to achieve for a number of years. When I was younger I didn't think I had a chance of playing for my country; then, with time and experience, I came to realise that I was good enough and aimed higher. In 1988 the selectors denied me the chance of attaining my goal. No one enjoys having their hopes dashed.

I was deep in the dumps for a couple of weeks, especially when the boys flew out. But I realised there was nothing I could do about it, and I just had to get over my disappointment and continue on. I watched the games on TV, and had pangs, thinking, 'Gee, it'd be great to be there.' Maybe, I thought, next year.

In the meantime, my mates rallied around. Tommy had told them what had happened to me and that I was hurting, so for the next few months whenever we got together for a few off-season drinks they'd all start singing 'Leaving On A Jet Plane'. Yes, they were having a go at me, as mates do, but they were also letting me know that they understood what I was going through.

5
GOING UNDERCOVER

It says a great deal about rugby's profile back in the '80s, as opposed to today, that even while I was playing for Queensland and in the best club team in the state I could still work for two and a half years from 1987–89 as a 'covert operative'. In layman's terms, an undercover cop. I had to master the art of blending in with drug dealers, break-and-enter merchants and assorted thieves who are attracted to the lights of the seedy side of the Gold Coast. Can you imagine rugby league's Shane Webcke or Gorden Tallis getting away with that?

To pull it off entailed convincingly passing myself off as a crook or a drug dealer. Like an actor, I had to *become* a drug dealer or receiver of stolen property, just like the blokes I was mixing with and arresting. My life depended on my identity remaining a secret. If my cover was blown it could have had fatal results for me.

Basically, it's a fine and dangerous line an undercover cop has to tread. You hang around and ingratiate yourself with the convicted criminals, try to make them think you're just like them, get introduced to other thieves and dealers, infiltrate, then, once you've won their confidence, get invited on jobs, which meant perhaps doing a break and enter, buying the stolen goods and setting the lawbreakers up for an arrest. I learned to fly by the seat of my pants with my life always at risk.

When I was first sounded out about going undercover, they asked me whether my rugby career would be a problem and I assured them it wouldn't because I had only started playing first grade and had no idea I'd make it to the big time. When I began getting picked in the representative sides I was already ensconced in my world of seedy Gold Coast nightclubs and bars. It was only when I was selected for the Wallabies in 1989 that my profile got too high and I was plucked out of the danger zone.

I still believe it was some kind of miracle that I pulled off my undercover stint. I suppose I was lucky that none of the criminals I was mixing with were rugby fans. I took precautions, too. I changed my appearance regularly. Mullets, rat's tails, beards, big and small moustaches, earrings, buzzcuts, sideburns, goatees – I sported them all in various combinations, to the amusement of my rugby teammates. Like the blokes I had to mix with, I'd wear the same pair of jeans, shoes and T-shirt for months on end. This clothing became my uniform.

When I was on the job I underwent a Jekyll and Hyde-style personality transformation. Criminals, I discovered, are different from ordinary people. They have a set of values that's alien, thank goodness, to most of us. I learned early on that to have credibility, I had to act and think like one. That meant getting the small details right. Basic respect for others and social responsibility wasn't high on the agenda. Most criminals are almost totally self focused. Saying 'Please' or 'Thank you' was a rarity, you made sure you were never seen reading a newspaper or a book, and when my druggie 'mates' and I hit the fast-food shops I did what they did and threw the burger and fried chicken wrappers straight onto the ground or out of the car window. They don't care much about keeping the streets litter-free and anyone who does they think is weird. Ladies first through a door or an elevator was just not done, and I needed to instinctively learn to shuffle into a doorway, lane or shop so as not to be noticed when the police drove by. For 20 years I had been taught right from wrong, good from bad, respect from disrespect, and now in a matter of weeks and months I had to change that ingrained philosophy.

I had to invent a new me. It was vital to create a plausible history for myself, remember it so I didn't get caught up in my own fabrications, and stick to it at all times. It had to be as close to the truth as possible, so I never got out of my depth. I rehearsed my story – things like where I had grown up, where I had worked. In the undercover game you don't say you have been to jail unless you have because it would be too easy to come unstuck. If an undercover policeman says he has worked as a mechanic he had better know how to fix a car because there'll come a time when he'll be called on and if he can't do the business he'll be revealed as a liar and that could cost him his life. For instance, I said I'd been employed as a concrete form worker and that I'd been a service station attendant, and earlier in my life I had been both of these. Not for long but enough to be able to talk the talk. You stay close to the truth because on the occasions that you are with your new friends and not fully with it – too much dope, too many beers – you need to be able to hang on to that thread of truth.

I called myself 'Dan Page'. It was important to retain my Christian name, just in case someone who knew me caught me by surprise and called me 'Dan', so I'd still be sweet. Obviously, if I was going by the name of 'Bob' I'd be in deep trouble.

Tommy Lawton recalls when he happened into a bar one day when I was in my working mode: 'Dan was with all these idiots in a bar and one of the guys in the crowd recognised him and called out to him and because Crowley was working, this wasn't a flash idea. So the guy's come over and before he could open his mouth, Dan's just dropped him. The bloke got off the ground and Dan said, "Oh, sorry, mate. I must've got the wrong bloke . . . " or whatever, and left. But that was how Crowls alleviated the problem, by just dropping the guy. I don't know whether he caught up with him later to apologise. I think it was pretty common knowledge among all his friends to ignore Crowley if he was working, that's for sure.'

The level of paranoia within the criminal ranks was amazing. Everyone was suspected of being a 'narc', an undercover cop. It was amusing to be in a conversation where three or four associates would be discussing how they thought this or that person was a cop, and the way the inner workings of a drug-affected mind came up with that hypothesis. Unfortunately, midway through the Gold Coast job they began hypothesising about me. Unbeknown to me, one of the dealers from whom I'd been buying quantities of heroin owed a substantial amount of money to his supplier. As usual, this fellow, whose name was Paul, had used more than he had sold and was in the red to the order of 10 grand. In his mind the best way to divert attention from himself was to finger someone as a cop – then all eyes would be off him and on that person. The debt wouldn't go away but by creating suspicion Paul would be buying time to sell more and recoup the loss. He picked me as the dummy. Hundreds of blokes to choose from and he decides on me. Later I would find that he had no reason to start rumours about me, he just needed a scapegoat and I was the one.

Word started to spread that I was an undercover cop, and soon the only one who would deal with me was my main target, a fellow named Trevor. He was happy to stick with me, as I had helped him out on a few occasions and he simply didn't believe I was a police officer. He also knew that Paul was deeply in debt and would have been trying to deflect the heat.

To try to save the situation I did what any of the other baddies would do and started mouthing off that I was going to get my accuser. Until then I would see Paul every day, but suddenly I couldn't find him anywhere. My work was suffering. He was obviously giving me a wide berth. Every time I left the old Birdwatcher's Bar on the Surfers Paradise Mall where we used to meet, he would show up 10 minutes later. Finally, I worked out that he knew where I parked my van and waited until I drove away.

After a week, I'd had enough of this and knew I had to confront Paul to get it out in the open in front of the other dealers and users to clear my name from the worst slur in the drug trade – that of being a narc. At that stage the police had placed another covert operative into the Gold Coast scene. We would run across each other, a nod here, a wink there, but never really associated. He had his circle to infiltrate and I had mine. But on this occasion I organised with him to give me a call if he saw my accuser arrive at the hotel.

It was a Wednesday afternoon, around 4, that I left the Birdwatcher's Bar and then five minutes later my colleague called to tell me that Paul had returned. I did a U-turn and headed for a confrontation. Paul was a big unit for a junkie. Over 190 centimetres, he towered above me and was fairly solid, but was not fit or agile due to the ravages of heroin. I entered the bar and spotted my accuser. I walked up to him pointing and yelling, 'I've got fuckin' business with you.' Paul must have thought that attack was his best defence. He marched towards me, throwing his empty pot glass at me. The glass whizzed over my head – I said I was short – and smashed somewhere behind me. Paul continued on, fists swinging. What could I do other than retaliate? As is the case with most pub brawls it only lasted a minute or so with tables, chairs and glasses flying everywhere. I'm sure Paul was pretty well doped up as he didn't really come close to the mark, and I was able to land two or three neat ones on him. As we fought and wrestled I kept one eye on the others in the room. I wasn't sure if they had come to believe that I was a cop. Would they gang up on me? To my relief they stood back.

Bouncers appeared and dragged me out the front of the bar while hauling Paul to the rear. Next minute, still all pumped up and adrenalin flowing, I was out in the afternoon sunshine. I thought it was over.

To get to my car I had to walk through the arcade to the side and rear of the hotel. I figured I could go home with my job having been well completed. I had got the point across that I didn't take kindly to the inferences Paul had made. But as I walked through the arcade, to my surprise the bouncers manhandled Paul, blood trickling from his nose, out the rear exit and into my path. As soon as he saw me again, he rushed me.

This was neither the time nor the place to negotiate. Again, a few well-directed shots felled him. A couple of the other dealers who had followed us from the bar yelled that Paul deserved what he was getting for the accusations he had made and also that he didn't pay his debts. They urged me to keep beating him.

When Paul tried to regain his feet I let loose a few kicks to his midriff. This totally went against the grain. Here I was doing the kind of thing I would arrest another person for.

Nearby was an elderly couple in their mid-70s window shopping. They witnessed the confrontation and were screaming at me to leave Paul alone. I could hear them in between the yells of the other dealers pushing me to finish him off. I looked into the horrified eyes of the elderly lady, who may have feared that I would attack her next. I stopped kicking Paul, who had given up the fight, and walked off. As I drove down the highway I had an overwhelming feeling of remorse, not just for what I had done to Paul, but also for the everlasting image I had left in the minds of the elderly couple.

I must admit I did get a little satisfaction the following day when Paul approached me, his face and ego bruised, in front of a couple of associates to apologise. 'Mate,' he said,

'I'm so fuckin' sorry I called you a dog . . . I just owed some money and . . . I know it's the worst thing I could call ya, but you know, hey,' he pleaded. 'Yeah, that's sweet, mate,' I replied. And what made it sweeter was that I had a tape running recording the incriminating conversation.

The trickiest part was the actual drug-taking. You can't expect to be accepted as a junkie if you're never seen taking drugs. I smoked dope in the line of duty, but managed to avoid shooting up heroin. Again, I don't know how I got away with it. I'd go to see my local doctor and have him puncture my arms with needles, so I had track marks I made sure the criminals saw. The inference was enough. Heroin, like most narcotics, is a lonely, soul-destroying drug. Junkies always accepted what I'd told them and got straight on to the more pressing business – the only business that really matters to them – of injecting the dope into their veins. A druggie's life revolves around getting money any way they can, buying the gear, getting it into them, and returning to paradise. It's not like buying a carton of beer, cracking one each and sitting back to have a chat. You got your gear, you left, you did your business in solitude. For me, I purported to buy, use a little, and sell the rest for profit.

One of the real dangers of being an undercover policeman in the drug world is that you run the risk of becoming addicted yourself. It's simply another occupational hazard. To win the confidence of junkies and dealers you have to use in front of them. I smoked a lot of dope in the line of duty but, as I explained earlier, I got away with not shooting up by being crafty and just plain lucky. I didn't become addicted, but I've known police who have and destroyed not just their careers but their lives as well. There was an officer I knew who found that the urge to know what paradise junkies went to when they shot up was too strong. He took drugs in the line of duty, became addicted and soon was taking them in his downtime too. To pay for his addiction he started committing armed hold-ups. After being caught he received a hefty sentence and may still be in jail. Today the police have worked extremely hard with the training of covert officers and random drug tests are a way of life. Unfortunately, these are a little late for that officer.

Being undercover is a dangerous life. The people I had to deal with were usually society's worst. Most had done multiple stretches in prison, they were boofed up on heroin, and, like all junkies, were paranoid, not a little out of their minds, and would do absolutely anything to anyone to score drugs or to keep themselves from being caught. Their minds ticked over at a million miles an hour. I would organise something with them but they'd keep changing their minds, switching from Plan A to Plan B and then to Plan C and back to Plan A again. I would be sitting with them and they'd say, 'How are we going to get some money for gear? We're going to have to do a stick-up. Where? No we can't do it there because there's too much heat around. When? Now or tomorrow? Who's got weapons? Maybe we should do it in Sydney. Or Coffs Harbour. Dan, you're driving . . .' Through all this I would be pretending to be one of them, while trying to find the location of the stick-up, the time and date, how many guns they'd have and what kind. I'd also, without raising their suspicions, be trying to subtly talk them out of an armed hold-up. If a police officer or a member of the public was killed and I knew the hold-up was taking place, I could find myself in serious strife. I had to weigh up catching these criminals against the safety of the innocent. I had to try to remain cool and stay on top of the job, all the while knowing that if I was sprung I was a dead man.

Informants are a funny mob. Often they're worse than the fellows they are helping you catch. Of course, they're not supposed to commit crimes while they're working with the police, giving information in return for a lenient sentence, but often they can't help themselves. And they're always hitting on you for money. One ripped me off badly once. He tricked me out of $2000 of the Queensland Police Force's cash. The best idea is to have the informant make the necessary introductions with your quarries and then cut ties quickly. Give him as little chance as possible to mess things up.

Another occupational hazard was being beaten up and hassled by police officers who didn't know I was working undercover and who saw me hanging out with the baddies. I had to take it on the chin without complaint. And when the police questioned me, I had to remember to answer in grunts and monosyllables like the rest of the blokes.

To protect me and my identity, the Queensland Rugby Union and Souths management, my teammates and the television and print media maintained a conspiracy of silence on a massive scale. Amazingly, it worked. In all the time I was undercover, I was a faceless man. No photo of me was ever published in any newspaper or program. No mention was ever made that I was a police officer of any description. My occupation in pen portraits in football programs was always blank. In televised games my name was never mentioned. (I was lucky that as a tight-head prop I was usually buried in a scrum or a ruck and not a high-profile fullback or winger!) None of my friends ever gave me away, not even when they were on the grog. Even the fans who for whatever reason had come to know my true occupation said nothing. They all realised what was at stake. My life and my loved ones'.

Tommy Lawton recalls my predicament. 'We were all aware that he was working undercover. And at Souths there were a lot of exceptions that we had to make for Dan because in those days the club competition was quite strong and we were doing very well, winning competitions, so there was a fair bit of media interest in the team and especially in our good new young players like Dan. But because he was an undercover cop he had to make sure he was never photographed. So every time a cameraman turned up to take our picture Dan had to vanish.'

Sam Scott-Young also retains vivid memories of the way it was in those days: 'One time I took my father and brother for a beer at the Broadbeach Hotel. We walked in and there was Dan standing over in the corner with all these bikies – long hair, tattoos and earrings, and being very loud. I told my brother not to approach him because he was obviously working undercover. "He's probably doing a big drug deal," I said. Anyway, Dan saw me and motioned us over. I whispered to him, "Are you sure it's OK to talk to us, mate? I figured you were working undercover with all these blokes." He said, "No, I'm here with my brother." One of his brothers was a big bloody bikie.'

It was Martin.

Some of those I was 'befriending' would have thought

nothing of putting a gun to my head and pulling the trigger if they had discovered I was a police officer. Many of these people were stoned out of their head half the time, paranoid, and they knew that if they were caught trafficking in drugs they'd receive a mandatory life sentence, just the same as for murder. So it was a perfectly natural thing for them to kill someone who was out to put them away for the rest of their days. What did they have to lose?

Some of the traffickers I arrested meekly rolled over and put their hands in the air. Others threatened to kill me if it was the last thing they ever did. My old friend, Paul, whom I'd befriended and then betrayed, tried to leap over the court-room dock when, sometime down the track, I appeared to testify against him.

I made a point of trying not to worry too much about how easily my cover could be shredded. I knew if I let it get to me and started fretting and looking over my shoulder every time somebody walked into a bar, my nervousness would quickly be picked up on by criminals, who seem to have a sixth sense for sniffing out infiltrators. Even so, my paranoia occasionally got the better of me and I had to work hard to control it. When I was haunting my Gold Coast hangouts I'd see a fellow looking at me and I didn't know if he wanted to sell me drugs, if I'd maybe given him a ticket sometime and he knew I was really a policeman, if he simply thought I was a weird-looking dude, or if he recognised me from footy. I'd get hyped-up and have to tell myself, 'Dan, stop being stupid. Everything is going to be OK. Calm down.'

Another problem was combining the life of a 'crim', a crazy, helter-skelter life of drugs, alcohol, brawling, junk food and late nights with the iron discipline and punctuality required of an elite rugby player. God knows how, but I kept my position in Souths' top team. Many was the time I turned up for training or games feeling a bit under the weather from all my over-indulging, and on a few occasions, when I was involved in a big arrest, I didn't turn up at all. I'd place a call to our manager or coach and say simply, 'Crowls here. Can't talk. Can't play.' They'd know what was happening and replace me.

My controller, the fellow who ran the undercover unit, was Detective Sergeant Kev Robinson, who is now in the upper echelons of the Queensland Police. Robbo was one who had the welfare of his undercover men at heart. He had to juggle the interests of about five of us operatives, which got complicated at times because our cases would all be at different stages, and he had to work to a hard budget because resources were limited. Robbo had a terrific offsider named Sally Diver. He liked me to phone him everyday to keep him updated and would get annoyed when I'd let a few days go by without being in touch. That was the nature of the game I was playing. If I'd been running off to a payphone all the time I would have come under suspicion and mobiles weren't the norm.

The way we'd work, I'd team up with a police informer or befriend a drug dealer or a gang, go on jobs with them, become very close, then do some serious business. Robbo would give me a wad of money from the police coffers to recover stolen goods to buy the drugs or the property. As soon as the transaction was made, I'd set them up for a bust, or use them to introduce me to other, bigger, criminals. This procedure could be a week, a month or a year in the making.

Not all the police hierarchy I had to deal with in those undercover years were of the calibre of Kev Robinson. I'm not sure if things have changed today – let's hope so – but in the '80s, for some, getting on in the police force, like any other public service, was all about length of service, not talent. So while I – and a lot of other police, too – was out there risking my skin, my life was ultimately in the hands of blokes who, while mostly lovely people, had no idea. They'd been promoted into positions way beyond their ability. I'd try to tell them about a sensitive case, or some problem I was encountering, or the need to spend time establishing my bona fides with the crooks, and they had no appreciation of what I was talking about. These fellows thought I could just go and buy 5 grams of heroin from someone then arrest him, without first having established my credibility and won the dealer's trust. Some couldn't understand how you could know a criminal for weeks or months and only know their first name. They expected you to meet, buy and have the person's full name, date of birth and current address by the time you left. Criminals, especially the good ones, are very intelligent. The drug use is what makes them drop their defences. The need for the deal. Only the low-level users and the not very bright are caught by a stranger.

In my undercover years my wife and I weren't yet married, just dating. I lived with a couple of long-time mates and sometimes she would stay over at the flat. It was in character with my thuggish, drug-taking persona to live with mates. I don't think I would have been prepared to do that kind of work if I'd been a family man. It was enough that *my* life was at risk, let alone other people's.

* * *

It all began when I put in my application to join the under-cover squad. They did some testing and I had to answer some questionnaires. Some of the things they asked me were ridiculous. Such as: 'If you went to a party, would you sit in a corner on your own, not talking to anybody?' Well, if you're a policeman whose job it is to get information you're certainly not going to be a wallflower, are you? So of course I answered, 'No'. And they'd ask the same question in the next questionnaire but couch it in slightly different words. Whatever I did, the bosses saw potential in me and I got a start as an undercover cop on the Gold Coast which was then, and still is today, one of Queensland's drug and crime hot spots. In those days there was a spate of break-and-enter robberies on the Coast, usually perpetrated by druggies who sold the goods they stole to fences and bought heroin with the money they received in return.

No one – neither the fellows at the coalface like me nor my superiors – were given any real specialist training for under-cover work. I was simply told to read up on old cases and instructed on how to keep notes. Then it was, 'Here's a job. Get onto it. Work out what you have to do as you go along.' You were given orders and expected to carry them out. Infiltrate this or that gang. Give us the inside information. Set up the arrest without your cover being blown, then move on to the next job. Over the past five years, it's changed. There's bet-ter training, and drug counselling and testing. With the advent of Workplace Health and Safety laws, employers, like the police, have been forced to take better care of their employees' welfare. My saving grace through that time was that I was able to bounce all aspects of a job off Kev Robbo, who had been an agent, knew what the pitfalls were and was always there to give advice. Sally, his 2IC, offered a compassionate shoulder on which the agents could unload the stresses they incurred.

Looking back, there *was* one test I had to pass, but that was the doing of my peers, not police hierarchy. Soon after I was assigned, I was approached by two other undercover cops who said, 'Dan, we've got to go and do this big buy of dope tonight. The blokes we're buying from are a bit rough and we'd like you to come with us to back us up if things get nasty.' I said, 'Sure, boys, no worries.' I was keen to get this new stage of my career underway.

That night I met the two other officers at the designated address and in we went, cashed up and ready to make the buy. Inside were four or five unkempt-looking fellows smoking bongs. They started talking about the gear they were going to sell us. But something about the scene seemed wrong. I had the feeling that the whole situation was being staged for my benefit. Then I recognised one of the crooks. Unless I was mistaken, he was a police officer I'd bumped into a few times. I dragged my two mates into another room and said, 'You blokes are having a dig at me here. What's going on? This isn't a fair dinkum job!' The two officers broke into smiles and admitted it was a set-up they'd staged with other drug squad police, who were playing the roles of crooks, to see how I'd go. By agreeing to join them in what seemed a dangerous job in the first place and then sussing out it was all an act, I passed my test with flying colours.

Years later, when I was working with Robbo on teaching the ropes to other undercover operatives, he began to set up formal training to try to prepare them for the life-or-death situations they'd inevitably find themselves in. We even sent some to some faked buys, like the one I attended, and watched the young blokes as their sphincter-muscles started telling them that they were in deep trouble.

One of my first cases was infiltrating a family of thieves (well known to the Brisbane suburban police), who were on the rampage throughout Brisbane, doing an extraordinary number, into the hundreds, of break-ins at houses and factories. The police had a rough idea who they were but for months couldn't catch them red-handed. These guys were fearless and out of control. Then came a break. An associate of the gang was apprehended, and in return for a lighter sentence, he agreed to inform on his partners in crime. With his introduction, I was able to convince the family I was a crook just like them and they invited me to accompany them on a number of jobs.

One of the most frightening things that ever happened to me was when we broke into a house at Cannon Hill. We'd done a scout of the place and been told the family who owned it were away. In the dead of night we climbed in through a window and went about stealing everything in the house that wasn't nailed down. Then someone went into a bedroom and came out ashen-faced. 'They're in there.' 'Who's in there?' 'The fuckin' people who live here are in there.'

I froze. 'Please don't wake up, don't wake up!' I willed them because if they did they could get themselves killed. The thieves were hyped up, violent and carrying crowbars, and if the occupants confronted them I would have to align myself with the citizens. If I didn't and they were attacked and badly injured or killed I would have been an accessory. As a police officer your first priority at all times is to protect life, a higher priority than my undercover operations.

Thankfully, the couple who owned this particular home were heavy sleepers.

Another time I was the driver when this same gang I'd infiltrated robbed a shop in Ipswich that sold all kinds of electrical tools and equipment to builders. I parked the van out the front and the family piled out and did a smash and grab. They shattered a window with crowbars and climbed in while all the sirens were sounding. Then for the next 10 minutes they threw everything they could lay their hands on in that shop into the van. Meanwhile I was sitting there, my foot on the accelerator ready to go and hoping against hope that the police wouldn't show up. The last place I wanted to be was in the middle of the pitched battle that would follow. When the van was full, the thieves jumped in and we took off. At the first corner a car tore by towards the shop and I thought, 'What do I do if it's the police and they chase us? Do I try to escape and preserve my cover but take the odds on someone getting killed in the high-speed pursuit? Or do I pull over and run the risk of revealing my identity or, worse, getting shot by the crooks or the police or a gung-ho security guard?' That time, I kept going.

When I had accumulated enough evidence against this crime family to stand up in court and no other offenders were to be uncovered, Robbo organised for the job to be put down. This either came by way of simultaneous raids across the state or a buy bust. The thieves were arrested and sentenced to prison for a number of years. A few years later, after they'd all been released from jail, I was at the Treasury Casino with my wife and some friends and the ringleader of the gang approached me and accused me of being behind his arrest. I could have told him his own brother was the one who was the informer but figured that that would be signing the brother's death warrant, so I kept quiet and listened to this fellow's abuse for a while. As he carried on his tirade against me, I could see that my wife and my friends were growing uncomfortable. Finally, with a few rums under my belt, I'd had enough and I said to the guy, 'Listen, mate, you can leave us alone right now, or we can go outside and settle this problem.' He left.

I worked a couple of cases on the Coast and then I was assigned to a major job. A bloke named Terry, who was part of a break-and-enter robbery ring, got caught. Terry, who pulled off the robberies because he had a serious heroin habit, promised if the police agreed to go lightly on him he'd inform on the rest of the gang. He'd served a bit of time in prison and was terrified of going back into jail – more because he wouldn't be able to feed his habit than the prospect of jail itself. We took him up on his offer. The mates he was going to inform on were all drug addicts too, and the money they received from the goods they stole they spent on drugs. Terry, the informer, and I worked out a plan where he would introduce me to the other thieves, I'd hang around with them for a number of months, pull some jobs with them, and then arrange for them to be caught red-handed with stolen property.

Terry introduced me to the gang as a receiver who paid handsomely for stolen property. My daily education was reviewing the latest Chandlers catalogue and *Trading Post* to get a good handle on the price of electrical goods. Robbo introduced me to a friend to do a crash course on jewellery identification. This was my new school and to start in the game you needed a PhD in life. The crooks started bringing me their hot TVs, videos, cameras and jewellery. I'd examine the goods closely and, after a bit of bartering, buy them. I'd establish a rapport and chat to the crooks, finding out as much about them as I could without seeming too nosey. Then when they'd gone I'd try to remember what they'd told me, write it into a report and send it to Robbo. I found I was good at recalling what was said and done, and my reports led to a number of arrests and the gang of thieves was broken up.

That became my modis operandi: make friends with another group of lawbreakers and arrange for them to be busted before finding another band to infiltrate. A big part of my job was finding out who the other receivers were, too. With no one to buy their stolen property the whole set-up would fall apart, which is why in Queensland the receiver gets a heavier penalty than the seller.

It didn't always go smoothly. A couple of times, the villains did get an inkling that something about me was not quite right and broke into my house and went through my belongings, just to make sure I was who I said I was. I was careful not to have any remnants of my other existence any-where anyone could find them.

There was, and still is, an undercover demarcation line. Some undercover police targeted robbers, while others spe-cialised in catching drug dealers. The latter reckoned the former were the poor relations of undercover work. It wasn't long before I became a drug cop.

There was an undercover detective named Andy, who was buying heroin off a dealer named Trevor. Andy was playing Trevor along while he was trying to work out who *his* sup-plier was. Andy's modus operandi was to let Trevor advise the motel and room number where he'd be with his stash, then Andy would rock up and knock on the door. Trevor would let him in and show him the gear. Andy would haggle for some time; then, when they finally settled on a price, he would leave and return shortly after with the money to do the deal. Trevor had rat cunning. He watched carefully as Andy went about his usual routine and saw that he returned to the car to get the money. In this game you carry your money and never use the same routine. This happened twice, but the third time when Andy came to the motel and they were busy bartering, Trevor arranged for his wife to break into Andy's car. Andy had blundered by leaving his briefcase under the seat. In it was his buy money, his police pistol and all his paperwork. Andy was blown.

Andy was reassigned out of harm's way and Trevor charged with a couple of low-grade offences, but neither the pistol nor the money was recovered. As it happened, I knew Trevor from my undercover work on the Gold Coast, where he was one of the crims, and we were friendly enough, so I was directed to take over from Andy, find the pistol, nail Trevor and his drug supplier and the numerous peripheral traffickers as well. For all my credentials and desire to do this job, the police hierarchy said, 'No, you're break and enter. We need a drug guy.' Robbo convinced them that I was the bloke best-placed to do the job and reluctantly they came around to his way of thinking.

I pulled out all stops to weasel my way into Trevor's affections, but what really made me flavour of the month with him was when I saved his hide when he got into a fight with another druggie at the notorious Birdwatcher's Bar, a now long-gone establishment with a glass front on Cavill Avenue where drinkers sat and watched women go past and many drug transactions took place. Trevor accused the other guy of ripping him off, and the guy took serious offence. I stuck up for Trevor, telling his persecutor, 'Listen, leave right now or we're going to belt you!' The bloke took the tip. Between that and Trevor nearly dying in my van we started to get close.

After that, Trevor and I were nearly inseparable. He was of average build, with dirty, straggly hair and numerous tattoos, and a missing upper incisor tooth, and lived at Southport with his wife, who was an addict as well, and their seven-year-old son. Trevor wore lots of gold chains, given to him by junkies in exchange for smack when they had no money. He'd have bags of heroin, $20 bags, $50 bags, and I'd buy them from him. My scheme was for him to feel so comfortable selling to me that he'd introduce me to the other dealers, some real low-lifers who I really wanted to take off the streets, and I could buy from them. Soon I was an integral part of Trevor's drug scene. I got to be able to tell a junkie from a mile away. The big giveaway is that they do what I call the junkie shuffle. They take short, quick steps as if they're trying to make themselves scarce but not look like they're walking fast, and they're always glancing around suspiciously. I got to be able to fake a pretty convincing junkie shuffle myself.

Working drugs on the Gold Coast was one hell of an experience. There was so much buying and selling going on. Somehow all the druggies would know when someone was holding or selling drugs, and scores of them would materialise, seemingly from nowhere, all doing the junkie shuffle. It was like a feeding frenzy as the dealer sold his wares. Then he'd run out of gear and everyone would be gone in an instant.

I remember sitting in the Birdwatcher's Bar one Saturday

afternoon with some drug takers and dealers I'd pretended to
befriend, and all around us were the locals and holiday-
making mums and dads having their beers. One of the
druggies got up on his knees on a bar stool and yelled out,
'I've a $50 bag left and it's anyone's for $20! Just $20 for
best-quality gear!' It was like a chook raffle and the drugs
were snapped up immediately. A few drinkers saw it and
knew what was happening, the holiday-makers looked on as
if it were a doubles ticket in the footy and just kept on
sipping their pots.

I got to know Trevor well, and even stayed at his house for
nights at a time with his wife and child. I'd just sleep there
and then we'd do our business together. In the end, he got
life imprisonment for trafficking. Technically, the amounts
he was selling and buying qualified him as a trafficker, but to
me he wasn't really one of the really bad specimens. He was
never going to get wealthy. His main aim was to feed his and
his wife's habits. He went to prison for a long time because
police officers are encouraged to meet a quota of drug
trafficking convictions so the department looks good. Often
the charges against fellows such as Trevor are downgraded
after the statistics are logged. It's all politics. That said, real
traffickers, the ones who get rich by ruining lives, deserve to
be locked away for a very long time. Don't get me wrong,
Trevor and his sort deserve to be punished, I just want fair-
dinkum traffickers to get fair-dinkum time.

When Trevor was jailed I had conflicting emotions. He
and his wife were decent enough people. It was just that their
addictions had led him to commit crimes to fuel their habits.
He latched on to an importer and this bloke used him to
distribute to other addicts in return for drugs. I was sorry

that Trevor's young son wouldn't have parents, but then, I thought, what kind of chance did the boy have growing up with addicts for parents. And after all, Trevor and his wife were running drugs that were destroying lives. Also, on a purely selfish level, I'd put four solid months of work into getting myself onside with Trevor, and he had been unwittingly instrumental in helping me get in with other drug rings. I would miss him.

In the end, the drug importer who was Trevor's supplier did go down but, unfortunately, it was after I'd moved on. He was a typical fat, late-40s Gold Coast businessman. He had the tan, the chains, the flash car and clothes. He wasn't an addict, but he used, and sold in large quantities. This guy had a home unit on the fifth floor of an apartment block and kept his drugs in the conduit of the electrical box on the fifth floor of the apartment block across the way, so he could look out his window and keep on eye on his gear.

I was on friendly terms with many of the users and dealers, but I never got *too* chummy because in the back of my mind I knew most of them were incorrigible and would sell their mother for a fix.

Sometime around mid-1987 I'd been working pretty hard so I said to my girlfriend that I'd take the weekend off and come up to Brisbane, pick her up and take her back down to my unit on the Gold Coast (it was my fourth, I couldn't stay in the same place too long). We would have Friday, Saturday and Sunday morning together and then we'd cruise back to Brisbane at lunchtime on Sunday because I had to play for Souths in a Welsby Cup final (the play-off of the two top teams at the end of the first round of the premiership). I'd return to my undercover work on the Coast on Monday morning. Sounded like a good plan, and she was all for it. I was especially looking forward to a break from all the underworld characters I'd been associating with. I left my work van in Brisbane and rode my own bike back to the Coast. In hindsight I should have gone the other way, to the north coast.

What's that they say about the best-laid plans? Well, the Wednesday before there'd been a break-out at Brisbane's Boggo Road maximum security prison. Seven or eight prisoners, including murderers and rapists, had driven a garbage truck through the front gate to freedom, with one being shot during the escape. I heard about the big escape, but jail breaks weren't my area of responsibility so I didn't give it too much thought.

My girlfriend and I had just arrived down from Brisbane on the Friday night and were settling in for some much-needed time together when the phone rang. It was my old mate Paul, who, after our skirmish, was now on friendly terms with me. 'Mate,' he said, 'Oh look, um, err, I need to get hold of some money.' I said, 'You're out of luck, Paul. I'm not doing any stuff this weekend. I'm cashed out.' He was persistent, 'Mate, I've got a great TV and video here I want to flog. It's really Mickey Mouse!' I was getting annoyed. 'Look, how many times do I have to tell you that I'm not holding any money this weekend. Go to someone else. That's it, simple!' Undeterred, the bloke whined, 'But no one else has any money either. I really need it. I want to get some gear for my mates.' I yelled at him, 'So what! Tell your mates to go get their own gear.' He said, 'I can't.' 'Why not?' 'You know the boys who jumped the fence at Boggo Road? Well, two of 'em are mates of mine and are here with me and they're desperate for some gear.'

I just turned to my girlfriend and thought, 'Ohhh no. There goes our weekend.'

I called Robbo and told him what had happened and he said my first job was to find out if it really was the wanted escapees and set up their arrest. First thing I did was go to the newsagent and buy a newspaper because it had the escapees' faces plastered across the front page and I needed to be able to recognise them when we came face to face. I was fortunate that two Souths teammates lived at the Coast. I dropped my girlfriend off with them. If things went wrong, I didn't want her around. I asked my friends to take her back to Brisbane if I got caught up.

Next I phoned Paul and said I thought I could help him out with some cash for his friends. I told them they all had to meet me in the park out the front of Coolangatta Airport at 10:00 pm. At the appointed hour Paul drove up in a battered old Ford Falcon. Two shadowy figures were sitting in the back seat. I was waiting there for them on my motorbike. I couldn't have picked a worse spot for the rendezvous with these very dangerous escapees. It was deserted and pitch-black. If they got it into their heads that I wasn't who I was saying I was they would shoot me on the spot. My orders had been to confirm it was them, notify my superiors, and then the Brisbane detectives would organise the arrest.

I jumped into the front passenger seat beside Paul. He introduced me to the men in the rear. As it was dark I couldn't see who they were. I noticed they had the TV and video on the seat between them. Paul went straight into sell mode. I replied that I needed to inspect the goods. This was not only to see what I was getting but in the hope I could see if the two faces in the back matched the photos in the national press. Simultaneously, both prisoners lit a lighter and the glow illuminated the whole rear of the car. They were the wanted men. I said, 'I'll give you a hundred bucks for them.' They laughed, 'Mate, they're worth $200.' In the time-honoured ritual, we haggled for a while, and in the end they accepted $150.

The four of us chatted briefly. Then the pair in the back seat admitted they were on the run from the police and they desperately needed to get over the border into NSW and on to Sydney. Paul couldn't take them because the Ford Falcon wasn't his and wouldn't make it anyway. He didn't say so, but he'd probably stolen it. I knew I had to stay in contact with the escapees so I had no choice. I said, 'Look, for a price, I'll take you to Sydney.' Both looked at me and then at the bike. I answered the looks, 'I've got a van stuck away. It'll do the job.' One replied, 'Mate, we've got to get the fuck out of here. The cops are all over us.' I organised to contact Paul the next day to work out the plans.

I took off up the Gold Coast Highway, trying to balance the stolen TV and video on the fuel tank of my bike. I dropped off the stolen goods at my unit and then rang Robbo. 'It's definitely two of the Boggo Road boys,' I said. He told me to go through with the plan to take them to NSW. First thing Saturday morning I rang Souths' coach Gary Bird. 'Err, I'm in a bit of a spot, Birdy,' I said. 'I'm on a job and I might not make it to the Welsby Cup match. I can't say any more. You'd better put someone on standby.' Having to bail out of the match didn't sit well with me because I didn't want to let the boys down in the big game, and our reserves were playing a game too, so one of their guys would have to be promoted to fill in for me, thereby weakening their team.

Robbo duly called back. 'Dan, our plan is to arrange for the Special Weapons Operation Squad to pull over your van and arrest the escapees soon after you cross the border, but so we don't blow your cover they're going to have to arrest you too, then we'll square with them and they'll let you go. Sound OK?'

Well, no, it didn't. The SWOS blokes – they're the guys who, I liked to joke, dress in black and go round trying to kill people – were odds-on to give us all a beating on the way to the police station. On top of that, they knew how to shoot. If it was going to hit the fan in a gun fight, I didn't want to be on the losing team. There wasn't much upside.

It turns out that this time I was worrying needlessly. The arrangement I'd made with the escapees was on the Sunday morning for me to pick them up at the house on the Gold Coast where they were lying low and then drive them south. I turned up and went inside, and we sat around chatting. Meanwhile, I was trying to ascertain how heavily they were armed, and they were heavily armed indeed. But when it came time to leave, they hedged. They had changed their minds and now wanted to stay where they were until nightfall. It was a surreal feeling, sitting at the kitchen table having a bowl of cereal, toast and coffee and talking nonchalantly about travelling to Sydney with two lifer escapees while 500 metres away men dressed in black with automatic weapons were planning their demise.

It was a stand-off. Fifteen SWOS officers were on standby but couldn't do a thing. They knew where the escapees were because I'd been filling them in on their whereabouts and state of mind all night, but they couldn't storm in on them because that would have finished my job as a covert operative on the Coast, as I was the only one who knew where they were staying and all my criminal contacts would know I was on the other side. Every so often I would leave and take up with the Tactical group, apprising them of the situation and most importantly ensuring that all of them knew what I looked like and what I was wearing. I didn't want them getting confused if things turned nasty. At this stage I still hadn't retrieved my van.

Then came a stroke of luck. One of the escapees was hanging out for more heroin, and left with Paul to score at the Broadbeach Hotel. I went out and called my boss. 'He's gone to the Broadbeach Hotel. When he comes back, I'll leave the house and 20 minutes after I do, have the SWOS team barge in and arrest the pair of them. And so they don't suspect me, be sure to say to the fellow who went to the pub, "You shouldn't have gone to the Broadbeach Hotel because someone recognised you there and tipped us off."' My second call was to Gary Bird: 'Mate, I'll be right to play. Let second grade know.'

And that's exactly what happened. I was sitting on my bike, my footy gear all packed, waiting to get the call from Robbo that the arrests had been made and that I could play in the Welsby Cup final. But he sure was cutting it fine. The game was at 3.30 pm, and it was already 2.30. Then my phone rang. The escapees and my druggie contact had been apprehended and a cache of rifles confiscated from the hide-out. I was free to play. I revved up my 1000 Kawasaki RX and powered up to Brisbane. I wasn't booked, and I'll never know how. Maybe I was travelling too fast for the police radar.

I arrived at the ground 10 minutes before kick-off. I didn't even warm up, simply put my gear and boots on and made it onto the field just in time for the kick-off. I played on sheer adrenalin for the first 30 minutes. We won the game, and I partied long and hard that night. I had to wind down from all that high tension somehow. It had been a memorable weekend.

When the escapees faced court, their sentences were vastly increased, although they were already on life, and when Paul was arrested at the end of my job, he received extra jail time, too, for harbouring them. That's when he tried to leap over the dock to get at me when I testified against him.

These days I go to schools and talk to kids about the dangers of drugs. My message is that you can't know if you're a drug addict until you take drugs. If you do, and you have a genetic make-up susceptible to addiction to them, you're gone. So it's best not to take drugs in the first place and not find out. In my work, and among my family and friends, I've seen the damage that drugs can do. It's not pretty.

Addiction is no respecter of age, which as this story, one of the ones I tell students, shows. One day I was hanging around on the seats outside the Birdwatcher's Bar as it was too early for it to be open. A Greyhound bus from Victoria pulled up opposite us and a pretty young girl got out. Samantha. She would have been no older than 14. The girl came straight over to us and said, 'Who's holdin'?' Junkies *know* other junkies. It's like a sixth sense, and of course there's the old junkie shuffle. Sometimes the word would just go out that Bill, or Steve, or Sue would be back shortly and would be holding, so everyone just waited. I replied that Bill would be by shortly and he was holding. Samantha waited. Bill arrived and took care of her request. If it wasn't so heart-breaking it would have been bizarre. The girl and the fellow who supplied her took off together and lived in a flat on the Coast. She traded sex for his heroin. The final time I saw this child was six months later when we put down the job. She looked three times her age and had been in jail, and was obviously having drug withdrawal symptoms. She looked a mess. She was skinny and her gums were bleeding. God knows where she is today. There is an excellent chance that she is dead. What a waste of a life.

It wasn't all drugs. Old Eddy is still floating around the place. Back in my undercover days, Eddy specialised in sell-ing illegal rifles, handguns and rifles that had been modified into machine guns, so he made considerable amounts of money from criminals who needed weapons. It was decided that I should pose as a marijuana grower from up north who was in the market for guns to protect myself from criminals who wanted to steal my crops.

The first thing I did was to make Eddy's acquaintance and win his trust. That accomplished, I weaseled my way into his life. He was a paunchy, short fellow, mid-40s, very unhealthy, and neither he nor his wife were near the top of the gene pool, but he was cunning. Eddy lived on a few hectares near Birkdale, a suburb approximately 25 kilometres east of Brisbane city. As part of my cover, I lived for five months in a four-car-garage shed converted into living quarters at Sheldon, near Moreton Bay, about 10 kilometres from Eddy. That was my lot for five months, me and my dog Jake, living in this shed.

I wanted to establish a connection between Eddy and a number of gun shops whose owners had reported gun thefts but whom we suspected of selling them under the counter to Eddy and others like him. Remember, this sort of fraud would have been much easier to get away with in those pre-gun register days.

Eddy was armed to the teeth and had weapons all over his house and property. He loved his guns, and his great delight in life was playing with them. Usually, covert operatives don't carry guns because if the guys we were hanging with caught us with one we'd be exposed. 'What the hell is *that*! Why are you packing?' But when I was around Eddy I made an exception.

After seeing Eddy's machine guns, however, I realised that if I ever found myself in a violent confrontation with him, which seemed well and truly on the cards, I'd be at a severe disadvantage. My little pistol up against his arsenal would have been like taking a knife to a gunfight. So when I purchased one of Eddy's first converted machine guns I kept it as insurance. That made me feel a bit safer. I found an appropriate spot to store it, behind the front seat of my utility, out of sight but within easy reach. Later, as Eddy and I bonded, I bought more of these guns from him.

With money supplied by my controller Robbo, I inveigled myself into Eddy's affections by purchasing around 15 rifles, eight pistols, some with silencers attached, and a huge World War II Vickers machine gun that came in a case with a tripod and cases of ammunition. I told Eddy that I needed a gun with which I could pick off blokes way out in our marijuana fields. 'Mate,' said Eddy, handing me the machine gun, 'this'll mow down anyone within a kilometre.'

I also bought from Eddy a number of small land-mine devices. They resembled tobacco containers but had explosives inside. You attach them to floorboards or connect them to trip wires and if someone is trespassing and bumps into one of these they blow up, taking the trespasser's foot with it. 'Lay them strategically around the crops,' Eddy advised and he would lovingly teach me his trade.

Yet, despite my best efforts to get the information out of him, Eddy wouldn't divulge the names of the people he was buying his guns from and selling to. So he had to be taken off the streets. He was of no further use, and every day he was out there with his guns he was a danger to the community.

The plan my bosses concocted went this way: I'd enter his premises miked up and record him selling me guns while down the road a squad of officers would be waiting who would charge in and arrest Eddy as the deal was being done.

As usual, nothing went to plan. The microphone they'd given me to wear was faulty and the guys couldn't hear our conversation. Naturally, they jumped the gun, so to speak. Quite a few of them were constables who had only been recently promoted to detective and they'd had no real training to deal with situations like this. They were hopeless. As they advanced on Eddy's house, they were revving their motors and stumbling around in a panic, falling over and dropping their guns. I thought, 'These guys are more likely to shoot me than Eddy is!' Of course, Eddy heard them approaching, realised I'd set him up, and tried to escape. I grabbed him and he snapped. I was suddenly in a vicious punch-up with my old mate. I subdued him just as the cops burst in the door screaming and shouting and pointing their firearms at Eddy. 'Boys, boys,' I said, 'it's OK.

Everything's under control. Put those bloody guns down before you kill someone.' Sometimes, as I said, I was more frightened of the police than I was of the baddies.

Another highlight – if you can call it that – of my undercover career was when I did a deal with some druggies and thieves to buy what a normal user would class as the mother lode. A garbage bag-full of marijuana, good quality with plenty of head. Probably 4 or 5 pounds of the stuff at $1000 a pound. Actually, it was a multi-deal. As well as the bag of dope, I agreed to buy from them a brand-new Ford Falcon sedan they'd stolen from Casino in northern New South Wales and a quantity of butcher's knives and other equipment, including ham slicers, that they'd stolen from a butchers' supply shop. Talk about nuts, but my job was to buy anything if it was stolen. I just made up some story that I knew someone who knew someone who would use it and the deal would be done.

I set up a meeting at the crooks' place in Ipswich. The idea was I'd turn up with the money, inspect the merchandise, haggle a bit to make it look fair dinkum. Then, the deal completed, I would stash the drugs and the butchers' gear in the hot Falcon and return to Brisbane. I was due to be at training with Souths that night and I figured if I could do the deal pretty quickly I could be at the oval in time, for once.

The criminals had other ideas. After I'd bought the goods I was about to leave when one of them said, 'Nah, mate. You can't leave until you have a few rounds with the boys.' I had no choice but to oblige.

It was at times like that when paranoia kicked in. There I was, sitting in a circle on the floor with these hard cases – me, my informant, six Aboriginals and two white guys out

117

the back of Woop Woop. Some of them were armed, all had the potential to be violent, and I thought, 'Hell, I hope this doesn't go bad! Do any of these guys know me? Have I busted any of them before? Maybe they've seen me at the watch-house on a Friday night?' (Watch-houses on Friday nights are a zoo, with hundreds of drunks, addicts and cops milling about.) If any of them recognised me I'd be in serious poo. Out came the homemade bong to toast and seal the deal. The Orchy bottle, the pot smoker's friend, hose in the side, steel cap attached to its end – blackened inside from previous use. It was also in the back of my mind that I was outnumbered nine to one, and if they wanted to they could simply relieve me of the cash I was carrying and refuse to give me the dope, the car and the butchers' knives. There wouldn't have been a thing I could have done to stop them. They were popping questions at me and all the time passing the old Orchy bottle around the circle. I was getting very wasted, which made it increasingly difficult to remember the back story I'd created for the job. My heart was thumping. It was very strong stuff.

Finally, they decided I could go. They counted the money, then helped me load the goods into the Falcon, and I took off for Brisbane. The trouble was, I was so stoned I nearly had a number of accidents en route. I stopped the car and called the coach, Gary Bird. 'Sorry, mate, I won't be making training tonight.'

Not surprisingly, my job was taking a toll on me. Whether it was the life-or-death pressure of working undercover or me remaining in my undercover persona of a macho tough guy in my personal life, I'm not sure. But I was drinking too much and behaving badly, being argumentative and aggressive with my friends and my girlfriend, who wasted no time telling me I was way out of order. 'Dan,' she'd say, 'you're being a dickhead again.'

Make no mistake, you pay a price for being an undercover cop. That's why two years in the role is pretty much the limit. The longer you stay in the job, too, the greater the chance of your cover being blown, or of you succumbing to addiction, stress, or just turning into a permanent dickhead who thinks the normal rules do not apply to you. I laugh when business executives say they have stressful jobs and whinge when the boss tells them they have to have a report ready by Thursday.

I recall being in a dressing room prior to facing the All Blacks when our coach Rod Macqueen looked at me and said, 'You don't seem to get too nervous?' My reply, which wasn't supposed to sound heroic, just came out, 'Rod, when you knock a door in and you think the person on the other side has a gun, *that's* when you get nervous.' He nodded and walked on. But that type of nervousness wasn't reserved for me. It was the lot of every police officer doing their job.

6

DIFFERENT WORLDS

MEANWHILE, I HAD another life to lead, the one I lived on the football paddock, a world away from the underworld. And as the 1989 season kicked off, I was still coming to terms with my deep disappointment at not being selected in the Wallabies touring team to Europe. However, as it turned out, I didn't have to wait long to get on a plane.

I was picked in the Queensland team that toured South America in March, 1989. 'Dan is one of the young players to whom I will be paying special attention,' coach John Connolly told reporters when the squad was announced. 'I anticipate he will play five of the eight games. He is everything Australian rugby is looking for. It is Australia's declared intention to find props not only skilled in scrummaging, but mobile ball players in the All Black mould. Dan fits the bill perfectly. He is the perfect man to replace the retired Andy McIntyre. It is a tragedy he did not make last year's Wallaby tour.'

We knew it would be a full-on campaign. South American sides are traditionally strong in the forwards with powerful and skilled scrummagers such as Test stars of the day Serafin Dengra, who would later come to play in Queensland, and Diego Cash.

Also, the Chile Invitation XV we'd be playing was full of South Africans playing in South America while the Springboks, because of the South African government's apartheid policy, were persona non grata in international rugby. And we had a date with Tucuman, a ferociously physical team and the No. 1 provincial side in Argentina. They'd played a draw with France the year before in a match so violent that Tucuman was banned for playing for six months. Cuyo would also be a hurdle, and Buenos Aires comprised a number of blokes from the Argentinean Pumas side.

Our squad was a mix of old heads like Mark McBain, Michael Lynagh, our skipper Bill Campbell and Peter Grigg, and novices in the maroon jumper such as Jason Little, Sam Scott-Young, Brendan Nasser, Paul Carozza, Anthony Herbert, Richard Tombs and myself.

There was a bit of a furore when our coach John Connolly, who'd succeeded Bob Templeton, and manager John Breen announced we wouldn't play against the Chile Invitation team because they planned to field more than the International Rugby Board's limit of seven South Africans – any more supposedly constituted a South African international side. We players couldn't have cared less how many Springboks were in the team. I was sitting around having a few drinks with the guys when we were joined by some journalists covering the tour. In what was nothing more than a bar-room boast among mates, I declared that we really didn't give a damn if they picked 15 Springboks to play against us, we'd still beat them. Besides, I went on, you might only get one chance to play against the Boks and when it comes you should grab it. (If I could have looked into the future and seen what would happen to me when I took on Guy Kebble I might have seen that maybe I was being a little presumptuous.) One reporter in particular took note of my words, and a few days later I saw them plastered all over an Australian newspaper. I thought this was unfair, and it certainly breached the agreed-on code that because of my undercover police work I was to be kept right out of the papers. I'll let Sam Scott-Young, who was there, take up the story: 'The reporter knew he shouldn't have featured Dan in his story, but he quoted him in a front page article: 'Dan Crowley says, Bring On The South Africans!' This was not a good thing for Dan. Crowley was livid, and revenge was sweet. We invited the journalist to play touch football with us. Matt Ryan popped up a pass for him, the reporter ran onto it flat chat, not realising it was the biggest hospital pass you've ever seen. Waiting for the bloke just as he caught the ball was our captain, Bill Campbell. Bill is 205 centimetres and the media guy was not much more than 150. Bill had no intention at all of tipping him, he just – *smack!* – hit him. The reporter's glasses went one way, his legs another, his head another. And as he lay on the ground, the whole team crowded around him and said, 'Don't *ever* report comments made in a private team environment again.'

We beat the Chilean Invitation side – minus the Springboks who bowed to pressure and pulled out – 54–12. That match was our fine winger Peter Grigg's last match, and as it happened he had the opportunity to beat Brendan Moon's

Queensland try-scoring record. Coach Connolly made sure everyone in the side knew that and encouraged us to do what we could if the chance arose to help Peter break the record. With two minutes to go, we were flogging them, and Griggy had equalled Brendan's tally. The scene was set. Our backline was lined deep with Grigg on the end of it, champing at the bit to get the ball in his hands. The ball travelled from five-eighth to inside centre to outside centre . . . Grigg had an overlap with the line in front of him. Then, from out of nowhere, our opposite winger, Anthony Knox, flashed in from the blindside between the outside centre and Grigg, took the ball closely off his hip and scored the try. Griggy, who was not of the nicest disposition at the best of times, was not amused. To this day I still don't think he has spoken to Knoxy.

We downed Tucuman, too, after a mighty struggle. They really put it to us in the scrum, but we prevailed and Cameron Lillicrap, who was described by former coach Bob Templeton as 'the finest loose-head prop in the world', even popped their Test stalwart Luis Molina. Our only loss on tour was to Buenos Aires, 36–27, although we thought we played very well and our pride was intact.

It was an education to play against Tucuman and Buenos Aires. There was so much power in their scrum. To match them, Lillicrap, McBain and I had to push so hard that our eyes were literally bulging and bloodshot. That had never happened to me before and it happened only rarely after. Against Buenos Aires I picked up a neck injury that plagued me for seasons to come. Those Argentineans' strength was unbelievable. For them it was a cultural thing. They look on rugby as very much a manly pursuit. A pursuit of strength more than skill. We Australians are in awe at the skill of our great backs such as Campese, Horan and Ella, while the Argentineans' heroes are forwards. To an Argentinean it is better to win the scrum and forward battle and lose the match than the opposite. To lose the physical battle affronts their masculinity.

And so it was with the fans. The match against Tucuman was relocated to another district because the Argentinean authorities couldn't guarantee our safety. In one match the field was surrounded by 2-metre-high fences of razor wire. The crowds were going off!

After the Buenos Aires game, Lillicrap, David Nucifora, Bruce Davies and I wound down with a few beers at the after-match function. As anyone who spends any time in Buenos Aires knows, nightlife doesn't get started until midnight but Cameron wasn't waiting. 'Crapper,' as we call him, gets extremely playful when he has a few beers on board and that can be dangerous when you're dealing with a 120-kilogram bear. We found ourselves in a cab driven by a fellow who didn't speak English but who knew we wanted to go to the city's biggest and best nightclub, New York City. He also got the vibe that we were enjoying ourselves and in the mood for a good night out. Cameron kept putting his hands over the driver's eyes. The driver took his playfulness in his stride and started running yellow lights. Each time he did we'd cheer, 'New York City!'. Each light he sped through got a little more yellow, and then he ran a red light. Bad move. This time we didn't cheer, we screamed. He hit a bus amidships at 60 kilometres an hour. As anyone who has been in a car crash knows, after the initial impact it takes a short time to regather your senses. When we were thinking straight again, we realised that everyone was fine, but the cab was wrecked and we were all lucky not to have been killed. My head hit the windscreen and I suffered cuts over and under my eyes. The other boys had cuts and bruises. After checking that the driver was still alive we saw he was slightly trapped behind the wheel. He gave us the thumbs up that he was all right as bystanders extricated him. Then, because despite the accident our enthusiasm for a good time hadn't waned, we left the scene and Nucifora hailed another cab to take us to the New York City nightclub, where we knew some of the other Queenslanders were partying. This time we let the taxi driver do what he did best: drive the cab. Our assistant coach and dual union and league international, John Brass, saw us limp in and reckoned we looked a whole lot worse than we did after we'd been bashed up by Tucuman.

When you put 30 blokes on tour and add alcohol, disasters can happen. With us on that tour was the Queensland and Australian fullback Greg Martin, now a Brisbane radio personality. Marto had a streak of craziness that most people would witness after he played a game and consumed a few drinks. Anyone who knows Marto knows he has a rather hairy chest and he'd delight in setting his chest hair alight from the bottom until it burned up his chest into something resembling an out-of-control bushfire. After the Chile game we celebrated hard then returned to our rooms on the 10th floor of our hotel. To say that the construction standards of the people who'd built this hotel were below par would be an understatement. They'd used pieces of stick to prop up the concrete formwork, and each room had floor-to-ceiling windows with only a small 1-metre balcony. It would not have been hard to simply walk through the window and out into the abyss to your death. Marto, on his return after consuming his body weight in beer, discovered that he'd locked his keys in his room so he walked two rooms down the corridor to ours and with only an 'Excuse me', opened our window and strolled out onto the balcony and shimmied around a pillar separating our room from the next apartment, along that balcony past an unsuspecting couple who couldn't believe their eyes, clambered around the next pole and let himself in through his window. All this was happening 10 floors above the street. Many years on, I was to be reminded of how playing the goat while on tour with a few beers on board can have tragic consequences. In 2000, Michael Moore, a good friend from my police days, and a member of the Brisbane Broncos and then Melbourne Storm management team, was killed when he was mucking around and jumped into the Auckland harbour. Each time his name is mentioned it reminds me of how close I, or Marto or others possibly came to the same fate.

It was great to be young and playing for your state in a land as strange and beguiling as Argentina. Remember that it was just a few years after the Falklands War, and it seemed sometimes that madness was in the air. This euphoria may have contributed to the many incidents that took place on that tour. Sam Scott-Young always seemed to be in the centre of things. He's been dining out on the following incident for years: 'Travelling with Dan to Argentina in 1987 was an amazing event. Crowley and I are very similar in a lot of ways because we're both opportunists. When you're touring there's a heap of down time. Dan and I used to sit together reading. I'd be reading about how to make money from real estate. He was into books about investments.

Neither of us had any money, but we thought a lot about how we could get or save some. One day we decided to try to buy some leather jackets at the lowest possible price. We asked the concierge of our hotel if he could help us. Soon we got a phone call. It was the concierge: "There'll be a car to pick you up in five minutes." Suddenly we were being driven through the back streets of Buenos Aires and thinking, "Aw Jesus, we're gonna be murdered." We pulled up at this big house, the door opened and this guy was there to meet us. He was lugging an Uzi. We thought, "We're gone!" Inside there was wall-to-wall leatherwear, jewellery, china . . . the works. They wanted $20 for a jacket and, considering the average weekly wage in Argentina at the time was $10, we said, "Nah! Two dollars!" They said, "Fine!" So we got away not only with our lives but with our jackets and presents for our families too, all at the cheapest prices imaginable. Then, just when Crowley and I were walking out the door joking about how well we'd done, the guy with the Uzi stopped us and said, "You have to pay us a dollar before you leave." Crowley said, "Not a problem," and paid up. Later we asked our driver about the dollar. He replied, "No matter how well you negotiated, no matter how cheaply you bought those goods, it's important to them that they take your last dollar." The psychology of that blew me away.'

It was a wonderful trip, one of the best of the many I went on in my playing career, and a great blooding for we emerging Queenslanders. South America was exotic and interesting, and we lapped up the cultural differences. The only pressure on us was to have fun and to play our best. We succeeded on both counts.

* * *

In April, while still on a high because of our achievements on the South American tour, Queensland won the South Pacific Championship when we whipped Canterbury 16–6. We took three heads off the Kiwis, their All Black hooker John Buchan was popped twice, and I outscrummaged my opposite number, the 120-kilogram Tala Kele, who outweighed me by 22 kilograms.

Again, 'Knuckles' Connolly sang my praises. 'It would be an absolute injustice, a biased selection even, if Crowley isn't chosen for Australia this season. He has been the linchpin of the Queensland pack this year and I have no doubts that he is the best tight head in the country.'

Connolly's praise and the recent wins were well and good, but the acid test of how well I, and Queensland, were playing would be how we fared against NSW in May. Beating the Waratahs was one of three goals I had in 1989, the other two were: to be picked to play for Australia against the visiting British Lions (a combination of the best players from England, Wales, Ireland and Scotland); and then to make the Wallabies for the tour of France at year's end.

First up, NSW. We slaughtered them 31–3, and afterwards a triumphant Connolly demanded that all 15 of us go straight into the Australian side to play the Brits. NSW and Wallaby coach Bob Dwyer admitted in the *Courier-Mail* that our huge win had sent him back to the drawing board. 'Before today, any sane person would have had to think at least two-thirds of the Test team would have to come from outside Queensland. Now the whole thing has turned inside out.' Most satisfying to me was that our tight five – Lillicrap (who tormented their tight head Mark Harthill mercilessly), McBain, me, Bill Campbell and Rod McCall – punished our opponents in every phase of the match. One down, two to go.

The Lions that year had a wonderful team, a fact that became clear to me when they downed Queensland 19–15 at the start of their tour. I was unhappy with my game. We were up against it because our second rowers Campbell and McCall were less than 100 per cent fit and that was never going to be enough against the guys from the Northern Hemisphere.

Nevertheless, as soon as the game ended there were calls for my sacking from the usual quarters on the grounds that I was too light. Just when I was feeling that I'd be overlooked for the Test side, support came from an unlikely source, Bob Dwyer: '[Crowley] is streets ahead of any other prop in the country in terms of skills and work rate. His tackling, claiming of the loose ball and feeding off players caught in possession are outstanding. A lot of others are as quick around the field, but few are as effective at the breakdown.'

My fears about missing out proved groundless when my name was read out to play in the first of the three Tests against the Lions, along with fellow Queenslanders Greg Martin, Dominic Maguire, Michael Lynagh, Jeff Miller, Bill Campbell, Tom Lawton, Cameron Lillicrap and reserves Peter Slattery, Tim Horan, Isei Siganiyavi and Mark McBain. To tell you the truth, I can't remember who told me I was picked, I just remember hearing the news and then Dad and my brothers and me going to the local pub for a few celebratory beers. Camp was a whirlwind. Meeting the guys, getting fitted for our gear and blazers. Just understanding the honour of being selected for Australia, understanding what it was all about.

Among all the well-wishers, Tom Lawton seemed among the most pleased. After all, he'd had his doubts about me in the early days at Souths, and he overcame them and taught me much of what he knew about playing prop. He recalls: 'Dan playing his first Test match was one of the highlights of my life. To see this bloke who I'd known as a kid, and tried to help along, standing there before running on, shitting himself, trying to block everything out of his head so he could go out there and do the best he could . . . it gave me tremendous satisfaction. And of course he went on to play for Australia for a thousand years.'

It was a dream debut. We won 30–12, and to make victory sweeter, Queenslanders Dominic Maguire and Greg Martin scored all four of our tries in the Sydney Football Stadium triumph, which, incredibly, was the first time Australia had beaten the Lions in 69 years. It's always more satisfying to beat the best, and the '89 Lions had a number of all-time greats. Imagine lining up in your first Test against Gavin Hastings, Dean Richards, Finlay Calder and David Sole, who I propped against. Our scrum was the foundation of our victory, in spite of Tom Lawton and Cameron Lillicrap having to come off because of injury. When they went off and were replaced by McBain and Harthill, just on half-time, I thought to myself, 'Bloody hell! Here I am like a shag on a rock. Playing in my first Test and the guys I started the game with are gone.' I had trained for the last few days with Tommy and 'Crapper' and we felt very comfortable. Then Lawton says, 'I can't feel my feet. I have to leave the field.' Tommy was my safety blanket, the person I was counting on to make me feel confident that things were going to go right. He was replaced by the dynamic and mentally tough McBain. Then Lillicrap snaps the cruciate ligament in his knee, an injury that would haunt him for the rest of his playing days. He was replaced by the very capable Harthill from New South Wales. I confess that although I was unsettled by losing Tommy and 'Crapper,' the replacements did us proud.

The Lions surprised us by confining their attack to a series of high bombs by five-eighth Craig Chalmers. They persisted despite fullback Martin defusing them immaculately. Only when the game had got away from them did they start throwing the ball wide to their lethal wingers Ieuan Evans and Rory Underwood. Too little, too late. The damage had been done after we matched them in the forwards, some would say bested them, and then Michael Lynagh launched raid after raid in the backline.

It was a challenge finding myself the only remaining member of our front row as the second half got underway, but the new blokes settled in quickly and our scrum was as solid as Gibraltar. Our two second-half tries came directly from scrum wins. In the . . . errr . . . less technical aspects of the forward battle, fists and feet flew. We expected nothing less. I received an ankle injury in the second minute but there was no way I was going off. Calder, Richards, Sole and English hooker Brian Moore hit me with everything. In the early stages of the match I found myself on the wrong side of a ruck and Moore stomped hard down on my head. Luckily I had my noggin taped, which was rare for me. He would have really opened me up otherwise. They were a hard, physical team but we came away with a great win. After the match we were in a very happy place.

I went into the Second Test at Ballymore with a sore and

swollen head, thanks to Brian Moore's boot. We had that game – and the series – wrapped up when the score was 12–9 with just five minutes to play. Then the Lions, who hadn't been able to cross our line in more than 155 minutes of football, scored two tries, one to Gavin Hastings, the other to the dashing young centre Jeremy Guscott, who swooped when David Campese dropped a high ball – the second he had put down in quick succession. In the end, the Lions got us 19–12. It was another game in which there were no prisoners taken, a bit of a dockside brawl, and they gave us a mugging. Their prop, David Young, kicked our second rower, Steve Cutler, in the head and their forwards singled out our halfback, Nick Farr-Jones. He was repeatedly dealt with off the ball. It was my job to protect Nick and I went out of my way to give his tormentors a touch-up. Journalist Wayne Smith quipped brilliantly in his report in the *Courier-Mail* that with most of the mayhem being perpetrated by the three policemen in the British pack, the tourists were in need of their own Fitzgerald Inquiry. Funnily enough, our sole try also came from a dropped ball. Gavin Hastings fumbled a Lynagh bomb, I picked up the loose ball and passed it to Nick Farr-Jones, who scored.

After the Second Test, Nick, his eye blackened and his body a bloody mess of sprigmarks, went on about what a brutal match it was and the press moaned about how he'd been manhandled by the Lions. 'To me, basically, it's open warfare,' Nick was quoted as saying. 'They've set the rules. They've set the standards. As far as I'm concerned, if the officials aren't going to control [the deciding Third Test], we're going to have to do something about it. They seemed to go for a couple of players. We'll be ready for that . . . we won't sit back and cop it.' David Campese complained, 'We had been badly put off our game. The Lions had done that, plainly and simply, by intimidating us. They belted us and took us on physically, mostly in illegal ways. It wasn't far removed from blatant cheating . . . we had made the blatant mistake of believing we were going out to play a game of football.'

I didn't think the match was all that rugged, and it was nowhere near as vicious as the Languedoc game in '87. Sure there were a few unsavoury incidents. But I think Nick was just taken aback because the opposition hadn't treated him with such a lack of respect in a very long time. The Lions' tactics worked, and they won, and that's all that's in the record books.

Rugby is all about momentum. We had it in the First Test, and for most of the Second, but in the final quarter of the Ballymore game, the Lions wrested it from us. Their forwards got over the top of ours and paved the way for the win. As the crucial Third Test loomed, we were determined to regain the whip hand.

We failed. After the Third Test, which we lost 19–18, our coach Bob Dwyer rued, 'We've definitely got problems. The Lions were physically stronger than us. Their pack is as strong as the All Blacks.' Richards, Teague, Paul Ackford, Sole, Calder and Young monstered us, this time without resorting to back-alley tactics. We battled hard, but in the end they overpowered our scrum – winning one against the feed right on their line – and they took the ball from us at breakdowns. Typically, yet disappointingly, I thought, there were again gripes that I was too small, and needed to be replaced by a bigger prop for the upcoming Tests against the All Blacks.

We were leading 12–9 early in the second-half of the Third and deciding Test and had an excellent chance of winning. Then disaster struck. We were deep in our half when their five-eighth, Rob Andrew, had a shot at a field goal which would have levelled the score. We were relieved when the ball skewed wide into the arms of David Campese standing in our in-goal. Our relief, however, turned to dumbstruck horror when instead of forcing the ball, the mercurial winger took off upfield in an attempt to catch the Lions off-guard and threw a bad pass to fullback Martin which bounced off Martin's shoulder. The Lions' Welsh winger, Ieuan Evans, pounced on the loose ball to score the winning try in the Paddington corner of the Sydney Football Stadium, which became known as Campo's Corner. If Campo had not thrown that pass we may have won the game. Maybe we wouldn't have. Who knows?

I remember running back and seeing Campese's blunder unfolding as if in a slow-motion film, or a nightmare. I remember, too, Jeff Miller screaming obscenities at Campo who, even to this day, cannot tell you why he did what he did. If he'd played safe, the Test, and the series, was probably ours. We were all bitterly disappointed with Campo and his brain explosion, and the fellow himself was inconsolable. After the match, he got dressed and left the ground, seemingly in a daze. Driving home, he was booked for far exceeding the speed limit.

I still feel sorry for Campese because in the days and weeks that followed he was belted from pillar to post by the press and the public for what he did. It wasn't the first stupid and impulsive thing he had done on a football field, and it wouldn't be the last. But the great and wonderful feats he accomplished far outnumber the disasters. When there was a strong push to axe him from the Australian side, his teammates came to his support, and Nick Farr-Jones even threatened to withdraw from the side if Campo was dropped. David Campese was an individual, never a team player, and his daring individualism brought out his brilliance. He rarely did what you expected, and the opposition didn't have a clue how to read him. Ninety per cent of the time he'd pull a rabbit out of his hat. The rest? Well, his suicide pass against the Lions is a good example. And actions like that have given his critics lots of ammunition.

I get on well with Campo, even though I know a lot of people don't like him. It's strange. I'm the first to admit that I don't have a lot of patience, but I do try to find the good in everybody until they let me down. Campo? Here's a guy who did little else since he was 17 but play footy. He went from school to playing for his state and country; then he went to play in Italy, where he's lauded like a god. Same here. He was always surrounded by people who bowed before him. Things like having a barbeque or going out with mates weren't on Campo's agenda.

He has always spoken his mind about rugby with all the subtlety of a sledgehammer. He always has and he always will. He's not at all political. He brings to the table brutal honesty and he seems not to care who he hurts or upsets with his pronouncements. If you don't agree with him, that's your problem.

That Third Test against the Lions was the start of my roller-coaster ride with the Australian team. I was dropped for our next international against New Zealand the following month and for the next decade I was in and out of the side. I thought we forwards did OK, certainly we weren't disgraced. But at the end of the day the entire front row – Tom Lawton, Mark Harthill and me – got dropped, not just from the starting 15 but from the entire 20-man squad to play the All Blacks. I didn't enjoy being held partly responsible for not only that Third Test loss but also the series loss. We were replaced by Dwyer favourites, the rookie New South Welshmen Ewen McKenzie and Phil Kearns (who was dealt a fierce sledging from the grizzled All Black forwards, notably Sean Fitzpatrick), and my old nemesis Andy McIntyre, whose retirement had proved to be short-lived. The All Blacks easily won that game, in which Tim Horan also debuted, by 24–12.

In most of that early period with the Wallabies I was coached by Bob Dwyer. He wasn't into man management. 'You're in the side,' he'd say, or 'You're out of the side.' That was it, no explanation was offered. A month or so later, I was in New Zealand with the Wallabies, warming the bench, and I plucked up the courage to approach Bob. 'Can I have a meeting with you?' I said. 'I just want to know where I'm going wrong so I can rectify it and get back into the team.'

To his credit, he sat down with me, but then he reeled out the old 'not big enough' line. 'It's not about your play, Dan. You're playing very well. It's just that a good big rock will always beat a good small rock.' That was his way of saying he wanted the heavier Ewen McKenzie in his team. Maybe in the end I should have taken issue with his words, but in my heart I knew where he was coming from. I may not have

My Grade 2 class photographed at St Elizabeth's. That's me in the top row on the far right-hand end. You'd never guess it from my cheery smile, but the nuns made my early school years a painful ordeal. My friends Craig Senior and Adam McDonald are, respectively, at the far left and right ends of the second row.

Early footy days with Souths Under 11s. I'm at the far right of the front row. My mate Andrew Johnstone (who would die too young) is second from the left in the middle row. It was Adam (middle row, centre) and Craig (beside me) who talked me into playing rugby union. 'You're fat, slow and have no skills,' explained Adam. 'You'll make a terrific prop.'

I made the Australian Under 21 side and was joined by my Souths teammate and fellow front rower Alec Harries.

I was an idealistic rookie cop (front row, far left) learning the ropes at the Queensland Police Academy in 1984. I'm proud of my achievements as a policeman, but knew I had to move on.

Sporting my undercover operative facial fuzz, I packed down with hooker Bruce Spencer and my Souths teammate and friend Rob Lawton in the Brisbane vs Country fixture in 1987. When Sam Scott-Young first saw my ever-changing beards, hairstyles and earrings he thought, 'What a lout!'

The Lawton brothers, Rob (left) and Tom (with me at a barbecue), initially thought I was too small to be a top-grade tight head prop, but with their help and my determination to master the skills of the demanding position, I joined them in the Souths, Queensland and Australian teams.

When I got leave from being an undercover operative on the Gold Coast I took off as far from the druggies and the sleazy haunts as time allowed.

I was just too tired to celebrate when, in my debut match for Queensland in 1987, we beat the international-studded French club side Languedoc-Roussillon in a vicious clash at Brothers Rugby Union ground, Brisbane.

Forwards are a breed apart, but after the Languedoc-Roussillon match in '87 I showed that I had nothing against backs when I was photographed with our five-eighth John Mulvihill (in a Languedoc jersey). John is now the backs coach for Western Australia's new Super 12 side, the Western Force.

Below: I'd never experienced power like that of the forward packs we opposed on Queensland's 1989 tour of Argentina. After our game against Buenos Aires I swapped war stories with my front row mates David Nucifora and Cameron Lillicrap.

A prop doesn't get too many chances to use the ball, but I was always happy with it in my hands and ready to get the speedier men outside me on the move, such as against Canterbury Crusaders in a 1998 Super 12 clash.

New Zealand halfback Justin Marshall struggled to bring me down in Australia's epic 27–23 Bledisloe Cup victory against the mighty All Blacks in Christchurch in 1998.

Again the centre of attention in that unforgettable 1998 Bledisloe Cup series.

England's Martin Corry crunches me in the Centenary Test at Sydney's Stadium Australia, won by the Wallabies, as his teammate Tim Rodber looks on approvingly. It rankled to have to wear the original Wallaby jersey, which looked a bit too much like the blue jumper of NSW!

No prizes for guessing who won! The Wallabies party as the hooter sounds full-time in the World Cup final of 1999. That game against the French, in which I came on as a replacement, was bittersweet because it signalled the end of my international career.

The 1999 World Cup-winning Wallabies are feted by Sydneysiders at a tickertape parade. As I hold the William Webb Ellis trophy aloft my teammates, (from left) Ben Tune, Phil Kearns, Tim Horan and Owen Finegan, soak up the atmosphere.

liked it, but I took it on board. And Ewen was playing very good footy. In those days they didn't have the rotating interchange bench, you just had to sit there and hope someone got injured, and that's what I did. It doesn't sound the best, that I was waiting for a mate to get hurt, but I only wanted him to be hurt enough not to be able to play.

Bouncing in and out of the Australian side was frustrating, but I never stopped trying to wrest my spot back from whoever had taken it. I always forged ahead and never stopped trying, and somehow, sooner or later, I always found myself back in the team.

After being banished by the selectors, I didn't fancy my chances of making the Wallaby side to tour France at the end of the season. And, of course, the acrid taste of missing out on the tour of Italy and Britain the year before when I was sure I'd been included was still in my mouth. Yet when the names of the tourists were read out, 'Dan Crowley' was among them, along with fellow Queenslanders Tim Horan and Jason Little, Anthony Herbert, Tom Lawton, Michael Lynagh, Dominic Maguire, Greg Martin, Rod 'Sgt Slaughter' McCall, Brendan Nasser, Mitchell Palm, Sam Scott-Young and Peter Slattery.

I had fun, but it wasn't exactly a red-letter tour for me. On a stopover at Edmonton, Canada, on the way to Europe, I played strongly against the not-exactly-world-class North American Wolverines, then, turning out for the mid-week team against a French national selection side, I hurt my lower back in our 19–10 defeat. I wasn't in contention for the Test team that split the series against the French 32–15 and 19–25. The First Test was notable because it was the debut pairing of Horan and Little, who had grown up as mates on Queensland's Darling Downs and went on to form one of the most devastating centre pairings in the history of the game for Souths, Queensland and Australia. The 19-year-olds defended ferociously in the first-half and unleashed their attacking genius in the second, when Horan scored two tries after Little had done the spadework.

7

LIFE ON THE LINE

MY TWO YEARS of undercover work came to an end in 1989. Covert operatives are normally returned to a uniform job so they can readjust to normal police work. But I had the choice of going back into uniform or working as a PE instructor at the Police Academy. My friend, Bill Turner, was still at the Academy, and my international rugby career was also taking off then, so I figured the physical training at the Academy would be good for me.

Problem was, it was a profound shock to my system. For two years I hadn't had to worry, like blokes at the Academy do, about setting my alarm clock to wake me at the crack of dawn. I hadn't had to bother with shaving, shining my shoes, keeping my uniform pressed and clean or making sure my hair was regulation length. When I was undercover, I went to bed late and rose late. I might have worked 20 hours one day and only one the next, but I was doing an important job, one that helped the community by fighting crime on its own turf. What did it matter that my undercover uniform was jeans, T-shirt, thongs, earring, scraggy beard and a hoonish haircut? Punctuality was important at the Academy, but crims are *never* on time. Like a soldier returning from a war zone, I had trouble fitting into the sanitised life at the Academy. Thank goodness for my footy. I was a regular for Souths, Queensland and pressing hard for the Wallaby run-on team. It was only at training, at games and when I was with my teammates that I felt sane.

The other police and fellows like Bill Turner were great, but, from the very start, I was unpopular with some of the hierarchy at the Academy. I simply found it impossible to go from one extreme of police work to another with no time to decompress. The bosses there told me to pull my socks up, and I thought to myself, 'Get off my case!'. They were right but I was still looking through my old work eyes.

Thank goodness that just when it looked like I'd have to resign from the force altogether I received an offer to do more agent work: as a controller myself now. My job was to supply the undercover men out in the field with the money to buy their drugs and stolen goods, just as Robbo had supplied me when I was working undercover on the Coast. I was also there to give them advice, and to act as a sounding board and a friend when things got dangerous. I'd be close by, armed and ready when the big, dangerous deals went down. The undercover guys would meet me at a safe house and drop off the drugs and other goods they'd bought, and brief me on the progress of each case. I was integrally involved in planning the operations.

In my years in the force I grew used to putting my life

on the line. Even so, the following experience of a friend, in which I played a small role, redefines putting yourself in the line of fire. Or, more correctly, *being put* in the line of fire.

One night I received a call from an undercover cop named Mark, a good man and an excellent policeman. He is no longer in the force, for reasons you'll soon understand. He was working undercover in Brisbane and pretending to be a fence for stolen earthmoving equipment. He'd infiltrated the inner circle of a notorious gang of brothers who were stealing earthmovers from showrooms and building sites around the city and selling them. Mark and his controller organised a plan to catch the gang. Mark and the thieves would steal some Bobcat loaders from a manufacturer at Ipswich and hide them on a farm that Mark had informed the gang was his. Mark would then take the $18,000 he'd been given by his controller to the thieves. The police would, in due course, arrest them.

The job was a fiasco. Shortly after the gang delivered the earthmovers to Mark's farm and departed, police arrived. They'd been tipped off by a member of the public who saw the vehicles being stolen. The police impounded the equipment. Mark arrived home and was horrified to see the earthmovers were gone. He called his superiors who explained what had happened. Mark was understandably furious. How could such a stuff-up have occurred? Then things got worse. The controller explained that the loss adjustor from the insurance company, who was due to supply the $18,000 with which he was going to pay the gang, was refusing to hand over the money because the Bobcats had been recovered. The insurance company couldn't care less about catching the culprits.

Mark made it clear to his chiefs that if he didn't pay the

$18,000 the gang would think he'd ripped them off, that he had taken the equipment they'd stolen and sold it elsewhere for a second payday. They'd surely kill him, he explained in a panic. He phoned me seeking advice. I said the best of a bad lot of options was for him to either have the gang bail him from the watchhouse, or to go to the gang with a bail slip and spin the tale that the police had arrested and charged him with receiving stolen property then confiscated the equipment. That should absolve him of any blame, and make the thieves understand that he hadn't doublecrossed them.

Well, the hierarchy refused to place him in the watchhouse or give Mark the bail slip. They told him he simply had to front up at the thieves' house, say that when he arrived home he saw police recovering the earthmovers and therefore he had neither the stolen equipment nor the money to give them. From his experience with the leader of the crooks he knew this would not go down well. In fact, he repeated to his bosses, 'He'll shoot me on the spot.' But the hierarchy was adamant.

Mark did as he was ordered. Fearing the worst, he went to the robbers' house and told his sorry tale. He was right about the brothers' reaction. The eldest, who was the leader, left the room and returned with a rifle. Holding it in front of Mark, he said, 'This is a rifle . . . this is a bullet . . . ' and, in a rage, he loaded the weapon, cocked it and pointed it at Mark's face. Mark told me later what happened next: 'He pushed the barrel of the rifle into my face. I wanted to remain standing but he kept shoving me with the rifle barrel. I fell backwards into a chair and he stood above me. He placed the end of the barrel on the right side of my nose, about a centimetre from my right eye. He kept the stock against his shoulder, bracing the rifle from the recoil of the shot that he was about to fire. I could see the top half of his face and his hair above the rifle as he glared at me. The end of the barrel was so close to my eyeball that I could look up into it, and see the baffles on the inside surface spiralling their way up into the darkness. "Don't think I'm going to hesitate to blow your fucking head off, because I will," he yelled into my face.'

Mark's only chance was to convince this guy, who was in no rational state, that he was telling him the truth, that the police had impounded the stolen earthmovers before he had a chance to sell them. How much easier would this terrifying job have been had Mark had a bail slip to prove he'd been arrested? He had nothing but his wits and adrenalin between him and oblivion. He stammered on, as the fellow rammed the rifle barrel into his eye, 'I haven't got the money, the coppers were up there.'

He later told me, 'I had an incredible feeling of claustro-phobic desperation and terror. I was so close to losing my nerve and saying, "OK, OK, you're right. There *is* something going on. I'm a cop. I'll tell you everything if you'll only let me live." I'd been in this position for many minutes now and it became almost impossible not to mentally collapse and throw myself on his mercy. I waited for the blast, the noise, the flash in my face, and the blackness that would follow. I was in extreme shock.'

Then the thief put his gun down. 'He seemed exhausted by the situation, too,' recalls Mark. 'He also realised that if I was dead he would never get his money.' Reprieved, Mark thought fast. He said he thought he could still get the money for the brothers. He'd borrow it if necessary. The head robber finally believed him. He put down his rifle. Mark reckoned by the time he did he'd aged about 30 years.

Later, Mark was instrumental in trapping the gang. But he got no thanks from his bosses, the very blokes who had put his life at risk. Nor did he receive counselling for his horrific ordeal. Again, it highlighted the fact that people making the decisions didn't understand the job at hand. In the everyday world, a manager, say, of a furniture manufacturing factory, who gives bad advice might wreck a few chairs. In the world of the covert operative, a boss's blunder can destroy a life.

After six months I was transferred to the Armed Holdup Squad. They were a real good bunch, complete professionals, and it was a pleasure to be one of them. Sometime in 1991 I was down in Sydney with the Wallabies for a Test, and Tommy Lawton and I were in our hotel in Rushcutter's Bay watching the news on TV. Suddenly I was riveted to the screen. A notorious bank robber who had broken out of jail and been on the run was being arrested before our eyes. He had recently rammed police cars and exchanged gunfire with police, shooting an officer in the arm and groin. Now there was the robber in custody and the officers who'd caught him were all my colleagues from the Armed Holdup Squad. 'Bloody hell! Those are all my mates,' I yelled at Tommy. 'I should be there with them!'

I got to learn the psyche of a bank robber. Unlike druggies, who are ruled by their addiction and often act erratically, bank robbers are more methodical and cold-blooded about their work. They tend to carefully plan a job, then, after they pull it off, they painstakingly plan another and execute it. They just keep robbing until they get caught. Each new job they pull inevitably gives us just a few more leads about them and usually in the end they run out of luck. That said, most cases are solved not by clever police work but when a crook rolls over on his mates, or a member of the public sees something strange and reports it. I was involved in a number of arrests before being transferred to a local Criminal Investigation Branch on the south side of Brisbane.

I was a detective for a year and a half and I found it satisfying work. I was pretty much left alone to do my job, get out on the streets and make arrests. I kept a daily diary and always noted my arrests in red, as was required. I liked using the red pen and got very annoyed if I couldn't make a red entry each day or so. The nature of my work often took me to the morgue to examine or identify bodies. My wife, formerly my girlfriend who I had married by then, always knew when I'd been to the morgue because she said I brought a particular smell home with me – the smell of death.

I saw a lot of death in my time in the force. I always liked to think that my experience desensitised me to it, but I doubt if that was truly so.

One traditionally bad period for detectives is the week from Christmas Day to New Year's Day. In 1992 I was rostered on to cover the district from the Brisbane River to Woodridge and out halfway to Ipswich. That's an immense area. Because many officers had taken their leave during the Christmas holidays, there was only one other detective and me on duty, and we racked up 40 hours overtime that bloody and tragic weekend which saw 10 violent deaths in our region.

We started the new year with a call at 12.10 pm. A woman had been found murdered. Happy New Year! It went downhill from there. The next day we had to race out to a freeway where a car with two fellows inside had left the road and hit a tree. Both had been killed. Then we had to oversee a police chase that went bad. A squad car was tearing after two blokes in a stolen Holden Commodore. We clocked the stolen car at 150 kilometres an hour. Minutes later, the Commodore driver lost control on a bend and the car shot into the air, hit a pole and was torn in half. One guy was hurled free and ended up lying in a nearby yard with a piece of the air-conditioning unit stuck in his stomach. The other was also thrown out of the vehicle, hit the pole and was dismembered. He was 17 years of age.

A murder is always nasty to deal with, but I remember the killing of one man in his backyard was especially sinister. The murder weapon was a steel rod. It was all so very sad. The victim was small and 55 years of age. He wore thick, Coke-bottle glasses and, we learned later, because he lived alone and had few friends, his job in a factory was his life. Every night after work he'd drop by his local pub for two beers before setting off on a 10-minute walk home where he'd watch TV and go to bed before getting up and heading off to the factory again next morning. He would not have hurt a fly.

On the last night of his life, after he'd left the pub, this poor man crossed paths with an angry 20-year-old lout in front of his house. For no reason at all, this vermin, who was drunk and had been trying to pick fights all night, abused the older man, who apparently told him to 'Get stuffed!' That set the kid off. He went berserk. He dragged the man into his yard and repeatedly hit him in the head with the steel rod. Then he kicked the man and jumped on his ruined body until his Dunlop Volleys had turned from white to red.

It was nearly midnight on a Friday night and I had already worked the day shift. I had a game for Queensland against the All Blacks on Sunday and I was looking forward to sleep. Another case was the last thing I needed just then. When the man's battered corpse was found, the night crew were summoned to the scene and subsequently called a number of us in to assist. Coming from comfortable surrounds where I was all at one with my karma to face a bloodied, mashed mess was daunting. I'll never be able to wipe the image of the man from my memory. His head was flattened; it was twice its original width but half its depth. I could not believe that one human could do this to another. But I shouldn't really have been surprised. History is littered with the unimaginable.

With the sun now fully risen I hadn't slept for 24 hours and was still toiling with numerous other officers to bring the perpetrator to justice. Never too far from my mind was the fact that we had the Blacks the next day. I called John Connolly, my Queensland coach. The Reds were about to have a training run and go into camp in an inner-city hotel for the night before the game. 'John,' I said, 'I've been called in on a murder since last night and I'm not sure when I'll be free. Sorry to let you down again, mate.' 'Knuckles' sighed and reassured me what I was doing was more important, but to keep him informed and get to the hotel as soon as possible.

We were fortunate that leads opened quickly and the offender was arrested by late that Saturday afternoon. With him were a number of accessories who were caught trying to burn his bloodstained clothes. It wasn't until 10.00 that Saturday night that I finally arrived at the team hotel. Enough time to catch up on sleep for the following day's battle with the Blacks. I wish I could go on about the great victory we had but unfortunately we were up against the best New Zealand team in a decade and we went down.

A number of months after that arrest we were in court for the trial, when I started to get concerned. The accused, who denied any wrongdoing, had scrubbed up well. He had an angelic face and was well spoken. Butter wouldn't melt in his mouth. He was well dressed. He'd also just inherited some money and had the best lawyers. I saw the jurors look-ing at him and figured that they'd be thinking, 'Such a nice young man could never have committed such a terrible crime.' I could still see the apprehension on the faces of the jury. Would they be up to sending this young boy to jail for life? Were they absolutely sure he was the one who did it? As they pronounced his guilt they looked anguished. Then the killer showed his true colours. At the jury foreman's announcement his handsome face screwed into an ugly mask as he screamed and swore and lashed out at anybody near him. Suddenly the jury could see just what violence he was capable of, and a visible sense of shock and relief swept over them.

On the night he murdered the man, that young fellow was a time bomb. He could have killed anyone. You, me, our loved ones. I can't help thinking of older, better days, when the streets were safer. When I was young, innocent members of the public could walk around without a care. No more. As I write this there has been a spate of child abductions in

Queensland. There has been an increase in the incidence of robbery and bashings, too.

At the core of all this mayhem, I maintain, is a basic lack of respect for others. Also, too many people believe the world owes them a living and if things aren't handed to them on a plate they simply go out and take them. I particularly remember one drug raid on a house in a low socio-economic part of town. Upon our uninvited entry we found the group I mentioned earlier. There was a bloke in his early 30s. He had never worked a day in his life. There beside him on the lounge was his son, a kid of 12, who should have been in school. The boy told me to 'Piss off!' And in the kitchen was the fellow's own father, who had never earned a wage in all of his 50 years on this planet. These people were raking in welfare money, and the fellow I'd come to see had been committing crimes to supplement his dole. Among them, a hydroponic drug-growing set-up in the garage.

We live in a much more violent society than did older generations. I really believe that. I have a friend who was drinking in a pub, got into an argument with another drinker and had a broken glass rammed into his face. Whatever happened to people just having a good old-fashioned fight? Every blue these days seems to involve knives and guns. And a one-against-one stoush is as out-moded as jousting.

About six months after my undercover stint on the Gold Coast ended I had a night on the town in Surfers Paradise with my brother Martin, who was soon to be married. His best man, Andy, was visiting from England, a stocky para-trooper who could handle himself. Friends warned me against showing my face in Surfers, where I'd put a number of local criminals away and plenty of baddies and their friends now knew I had been a policeman all the time. Problem was, I'd had a few drinks and was feeling 10 foot tall and bulletproof. 'We'll be all right,' I assured them. Martin ended up with another group of friends, while I showed Andy the lights.

Off we went into the wilds of Surfers Paradise on a Saturday night. It happened outside a nightclub – I didn't see a thing. Just felt a fist slamming into my head. A king-hit. I went down, semi-conscious. Then about six assailants moved in and gave me the kicking of my life. They broke my nose, chipped my teeth and gashed my head. And they didn't stop at me. Andy dived into the fray, receiving a broken cheekbone and gashed head for his trouble. I remember rolling out of the melee and seeing him lying on the footpath, his legs twitching under the sea of bodies beating him. I collected my senses and waded back into the fight, only to cop another going-over as vicious as the first.

To this day, I'm sure the attack was a get-square by the local underworld, but at least there wasn't a knife or a gun involved.

One of the worst crimes I ever investigated as a CIB detective was the murder of a young woman. Her body was found in her backyard. It was an horrific scene. Her head had been caved in and it seemed certain that the murder weapon was four bricks, all mortared together, lying nearby and covered in blood. There was a bloody broom handle there as well. And that wasn't all. The culprit had also left his wallet complete with identification. When we arrested the 20-something man the next day, the story came out. He'd had a relationship with the deceased woman, but she had decided that she wanted nothing more to do with him. He was drunk and reacted violently to his humiliation. He bit her – there were teeth marks on her chest – beat her savagely with the broom handle, then smashed her with the bricks which he'd pulled from the garden wall. As you can imagine, armed with his wallet, it wasn't that hard to find Mr Stupid. After a night hiding under the local supermarket floor, he ventured home, where we were waiting for him. He denied any involvement until we found his blood-spattered clothes in his wash basket.

But we knew that finding the culprit was only the short-term solution. A police officer can't help ease the pain of the victim's loved ones left behind.

For some reason I always seemed to have a case at inopportune moments. And an impending Welsby Cup game seemed to be a signal for blokes to do the wrong thing. It was a Saturday night with the Welsby Cup final the next day. I was rostered midnight to 8.00 am in a uniformed car to patrol our area of inner south Brisbane. Although I was junior in rank I had a probationary constable (having less than a year's service) with me. I didn't know much more than he did. We had two crews on that evening and was hoping that it would be a restful, uneventful night. Maybe I'd even be able to grab a little shut-eye before the big game. My new and very keen partner was on to me about how he had come from the traffic branch and never had a drug pinch (arrest). I explained I had a big match the next day and said that if we got a drug pinch I'd appreciate it if he would let me have it easy for the rest of the evening. He eagerly agreed. And so we began looking for druggies. Within the first hour we stopped every 'undesirable' we could lay our hands on, but they were clean. Then, within the hour, we had one. His crime, about an ounce of pot in the glovebox. Not much, but enough to keep my friend happy. Off we went with our catch to the watchhouse. I led my partner through the processing side of the arrest. By this time it was 2.30 am. After I kept my end of the bargain, he agreed to keep his.

We left the watchhouse to drive the 3 kilometres across Brisbane's Captain Cook bridge to our station. Stopping at the first of two sets of traffic lights I saw an old EK station wagon drive across in front of us. I shot a glance at the passenger – he had long greasy hair and an arm full of tattoos, which was dangling out the passenger side window, but more importantly he had a face that had 'I am doing something I shouldn't be doing' written all over it. At the wheel of the EK was a woman, and, if anything, she looked even meaner than her partner. She certainly had more tatts.

I didn't want any more work, but couldn't help myself. Still, if I pulled them over on the bridge and if everything checked out, I wouldn't have to drive the extra 5 kilometres to the next exit and I'd have more 'z' time. I made the occupants get out and then asked them the usual questions: 'What's your name? Can I please see your licence? Is this your car? Have either of you ever been in trouble with the police?' As I was questioning them, I noticed a syringe on the console. 'Err, what's that, mate?' I said. 'It looks like a needle to me. Mind if I have a look through your car?' I told my partner to keep an eye on them while I searched.

As he did, I got into the car and started searching for drugs. Just then, the woman made a break for it. She raced right across the four lanes of the road, dodging oncoming traffic. I yelled to my partner to guard the male and ran after her, not knowing where she was going to run to. She climbed up onto the bridge's external barrier fence. The Brisbane River flowed 50 metres below. I followed her across the highway and stopped 5 metres short of where she was balancing precariously. She looked at me, she looked down at the water, she looked back at me. And then she jumped. I heard her scream and a splash as she hit the water. I considered jumping after her, then thought, 'No way.'

I quickly returned to my car and called for back-up. One minute later the place was crawling with police. Some rescue workers went down to the riverbank. The woman had hit the river bottom and badly damaged her back, but she was alive. The water police pulled her from the water and took her back to the wharf, where an ambulance whisked her away. In the meantime we completed a search of the car to find scales, bags of glucose and other fillers and a good quantity of heroin. All this neatly inside a doctor's medical bag with scripts that they had earlier stolen during a break and enter. I later learned that our two detainees were already on bail for trafficking in New South Wales and were on their return run.

We finally arrived at the Royal Brisbane Hospital to check on our midnight fun runner. The sun was starting to rise, and I had had no sleep. After a few hours' wait, the doctor arrived and declared that she had bruising to her back but would be OK. As with all attempted suicides, he stated she would be kept under observation. I explained to the doctor that it wasn't a suicide bid, that she was running drugs and jumped to evade arrest. 'Lying bitch,' he replied. 'Well, in that case she's yours.' He escorted her to the rear seat of the police vehicle. Both were then turned over to the local detectives, who were eager to have a chat. Our job was done. It was hitting midday and our shift was well and truly over. I never did get that sleep.

My next step up the police ladder of opportunity came when I was appointed detective sergeant and assigned to a police station in central Brisbane. I was back in the drug squad, controlling undercover teams again and also getting out and arresting drug traffickers. I raided hundreds of dealers in week after week of rolling raids. Bashing on doors, making the arrests and herding the villains into paddy wagons before bashing on more doors. We were doing 15 busts a day at one stage. Most dealers gave up meekly without a struggle.

The adrenalin got me through, but now I'm older and wiser I shudder when I think how every one of those busts could have been my last. There was me kicking on doors, and inside any of them could have been a desperate drug addict with a rifle. I consider myself blessed that I survived.

About that time I started having a few problems with some of my bosses in the force – just as I had when I returned to the Police Academy after working undercover. I'd spent so long living on the edge, risking my life, that I suppose I didn't take kindly to taking orders from some who, as far as I could ascertain, hadn't achieved much in their careers. I simply had no respect for them.

These time-servers and faceless men got their revenge by switching me to a nothing unit, a kind of Coventry posting where troublemakers got sent to be out of sight and out of mind. Then, adding insult to injury, I was told that I was being assigned to the Fraud Squad. I found this to be a total joke. It was a division where cops who couldn't even balance their own chequebooks were trying to investigate multi-million dollar crimes perpetrated by rat-smart white-collar criminals with university degrees.

It was just so typical of the wrong-headed way that they used to do things in the Queensland Police Force. Why not have trained accountants investigating these highly sophisticated cases, and use police officers to keep the peace on the street? The role of a police officer is to protect life and property, not shuffle paper. I'm glad that in the last 15 years there has been a change for the better.

It seemed that all through my police career I found myself pitted against a stupid and time-wasting bureaucracy. An archaic promotion system that rewards blokes who keep their head down the longest and stay out of trouble. Terrible pay, considering you risk your life every working day. Lack of support for officers in hazardous or stressful situations. Zero specialist training and post-trauma counselling. Police handing out summonses and issuing parking violations when they should be arresting lawbreakers. A judicial system that, it seems to me, favours the wrongdoer and legislates against the law enforcer.

My problem was that I gave a damn. I put everything into my job as a policeman. I was happy to risk my life, get low pay, and have little private life, to do a job I believed was worth doing.

Right then, in the first half of the '90s, my rugby career was going ahead in leaps and bounds, but my professional life was a mess and my personal life was, frankly, in no better shape. I confess that I was a difficult son of a bitch in those days. I drove too fast, drank too much, was usually angry. If I felt like parking on a loading zone I'd park there. Just like when I was a covert operator, my wife was losing patience with my behaviour.

Luckily, I saw reason. I realised that the frustrations of being a policeman were destroying me. I was retired from the police force in 1995, after 11 years of service.

I left because I wasn't emotionally right and I was angry, and I really shouldn't have been. Retiring was the easy option. If the hierarchy had heeded the doctor's and psychiatrist's assessments and tried to work with me to bring me out of my problems, I might have been able to stay in the service. But they didn't. Maybe they didn't want to. A number of police went through the same thing and also left. It was a numbers game. Train more police to replace the ones who leave. Even so, looking back, I think that I could have gotten over my issues with the police myself but it would have taken a little time and patience on my part. Then again, with rugby going professional the next year and bringing new earning opportunities into my life I might not have stayed anyway.

Resigning from the police force was both hard and easy to do. Hard because I thought the world of many of my colleagues, and knew I was doing a job that actually made a difference to society. Easy, because at the time my sanity depended on it, and I would be putting my future with my wife and growing family, a future I valued more than anything in the world, at risk if I stayed.

8

IN THE WALLABY
TRENCHES

THE POLICE FORCE and rugby . . . I was a glutton for punishment.

The painful neck injury I sustained against the fierce scrummagers of the Argentinean team dogged me right throughout the 1990 season. The debilitating complaint caused me no end of problems on what should have been an idyllic tour of Western Samoa in March. It reared against Samoa B, but I made myself available to play against the national side at Apia. This wasn't exactly the smartest move, because my neck gave me hell and I was forced off the field in agony. Nor was I the only one in pain on that tour. A few of the guys (most spectacularly, as I recall, Michael Lynagh), picked up stomach bugs and were crippled by cramps and diarrhoea.

In the amateur days, one of the carrots that rugby

administrators dangled to persuade blokes to play rugby, as opposed to rugby league, was the travel. In spite of attempts to get the game up and running in such places as Morocco, the Pacific Islands, Russia and the United States, a league player's horizons really stretch no further than New Zealand, and parts of England, France and Papua New Guinea.

In my long careers for Queensland and Australia, rugby took me to New Zealand, Western Samoa, Fiji, South America, the United States, Canada, South Africa, France, Italy, England, Wales, Ireland, Scotland, Japan and Holland. Playing rugby, sampling the different cultures and making friends – and occasionally, foes – in these far-flung places has enriched my life and broadened my outlook.

That said, there's a downside. I'm a homebody at heart, who has never really wanted to move from the area where I was raised, South Brisbane. And while I tried to make the most of my rugby trips away, especially for the first week or two, I always suffered from homesickness.

The rugby was the saviour, but you can only play for 80 minutes and train for a certain period, and the rest of the time I often found myself deep in the doldrums because of boredom and loneliness. Sure, Paris and London are wonderful and there's no shortage of things to do, but I remember one day in Swansea, Wales, Sam Scott-Young and I watched seven videos back to back. Anybody who's been to Swansea would realise that seven videos, *any* seven videos, would be more interesting than the sightseeing in that particular city. As they say, I spent a month in Swansea one day.

Touring memories . . . I have one of Sam on one of our Wallaby tours of France. I'm sure he won't thank me for relating it, but it's a payback for a few of the stories he's told about me. The boys had planned a night out, and then we'd been invited to the Adidas factory the following day to get some free samples of their gear. Not wanting to miss out on getting something for nothing, Sam swallowed some pills – maybe Vitamin A, I can't recall – which someone had told him prevented hangovers. At the pub that night, the publican brought out the biggest glass I've ever seen, filled with beer, and dared us to try to drain it in one gulp. We all had a go, and naturally ended up a little the worse for wear. Next morning, we took one look at Sam and knew that his hangover cure hadn't worked. He was far too sick to go to the Adidas factory, and as we left him at the hotel we heard him moaning, 'Yeah, bloody great pills, they were . . .' while huddled around the porcelain bowl.

The difference between a happy tour and a dismal one depends, by and large, on whether you're winning or losing. If you're getting knocked over, the boys get crabby and homesick. Coach Bob Dwyer tended to transform into a maniac when we were on the losing end. Generally speaking, even when things are going well, it's not the easiest thing in the world living with a bunch of blokes in unfamiliar places far from your loved ones. That's how it sometimes struck me, anyway.

Tensions are exacerbated, too, when inevitably the team splits into the Test players and the so-called mid-week players, or what we called the Roosters and the Feather Dusters. But whether I was a Rooster or a Feather Duster, what I did enjoy was the geeing-up that went on among the boys. Once Tommy Lawton was whingeing because he'd been dropped from the Test team and we were all were giving him a hard time for not copping his demotion on the chin. Then, completely out of synch with the prevailing mood, Julian Gardner turned around to Tommy and said, 'It's all right for *you*, Tom, you *deserve* to get dropped! What about *me*? What about *ME*!' Of course, we immediately forgot about Tommy and ganged up on Julian like a pack of jackals and didn't let him forget what he'd said all tour long.

Being stingy when it comes to a shout, or a lousy sledger, being a snorer or too messy or too often late, or a bad joke-teller, all can make life hell for a bloke on tour.

Often today when I catch up with my old touring colleagues, conversation turns to the times we shared on the road . . . and no one is safe, especially not me. As my very old mate Ian Cameron notes, 'All of Dan's friends see him as a very, very good target because he takes himself so seriously and there are so many things about him that are slightly ridiculous.'

Tommy Lawton was a regular touring mate. As he explains: 'Dan has a great sense of humour. We toured together in 1989 and 1992 and usually manoeuvred to be roommates, even though you were supposed to change your roomie at each new destination. We had great fun and I think it's a shame that touring players these days have a room to themselves. It's not as good for team camaraderie. Dan would be the unofficial treasurer on tour [being a Queensland police officer I wasn't sure that making me treasurer was such a smart thing – but anyway, continue, Tommy . . .] and I'd be his assistant, collecting sponsors' money from players and staff and other sources, and then divvying it up among the players. We're only talking about a couple of hundred bucks each, but in the amateur years this was quite a bit of money.

I was always trying to get Crowls to cheat. "Crowls," I'd say, "for every dollar you give the team, let's pay ourselves two!" But he always kept me on the straight and narrow.

'Dan was meticulously neat. It was a great joy to wait till he went out and then upend his bag, tipping his belongings all over the room, then sitting back and watching him fuss about, cleaning everything up. He definitely took a little getting used to as a roomie. He had some idiosyncratic habits, including a nasty one of being the first to use the toilet when we were assigned our room . . . and he wouldn't close the door. That was a definite Dan-ism.'

Rod McCall has now and again been known to remind people of what he calls my 'weakness for OP rum . . . On tour, I recall when Dan was under the influence he'd get a bit aggressive about sharing his good times with you, and he would always try to engage you in deep and meaningful conversations. I guess, being a cop, he didn't get the chance too often to break out and have a bit of fun, and Dan made up for that on tour. If you go to South America or France you let your hair down. He enjoyed his tours.

'The 1992 tour of Ireland and Wales was a memorable one. We were world champions and had had a successful year maintaining our ranking. I remember on the field Dan was belted from pillar to post. He was always getting opened up on that tour. There were also many light moments. We had a talent night, and one of the blokes did an impersonation of Dan. He covered himself in fake stitches, put on a blond wig and walked onto the stage on his knees. That brought the house down. Giving Dan a hard time was a blood sport. He took it pretty well, mostly.'

Since this seems to be turning into a Dan Crowley roast,

it may be the right time to tell you about all the nicknames I've accumulated in my career. Many originated on tour, when the boys have enough time on their hands to be even more cruel than usual. 'When I think of Dan,' says Rod McCall, 'I think of a short-arse, with stumpy legs. I used to call him "the vagrant" because he had no visible means of support.'

As Ian Cameron remarked, there seems to be something about me, and my lack of height, that brings out the smart arse in some people. For a while I was called Dan Dog after a cartoon character. That soon got shortened to Dog, which is an unfortunate name for a policeman, because a dog, in underworld-speak, is a police informant who rolls over on his mates. I also got lumbered with Poison Dwarf, Mini Me (the evil little guy from the *Austin Powers* movies), Mighty Midget, Garden Gnome and Barney Rubble. My mates are very fond of telling people, with a straight face, that I had done very well to play for Australia after overcoming a terrible childhood injury when I lost my legs below the knees in a boomerang mishap. The genesis of that was at the '91 Rugby World Cup. When I was a kid, I went to Mudgereebah with my mum and dad and learned to throw and catch a boomerang. Well, somehow a couple of boomerangs turned up at our camp in Wales and I picked one up, threw it way out into the gloom and caught it when it came spinning back. 'Whoa!' yelled the boys, 'do it again!' Someone cracked that I used to be 198 centimetres before that nasty accident.

Even when you're on tour and you visit places where there are wonderful things to do and see, being in a team environment doesn't exactly lend itself to quality sightseeing. You're treated like sheep. You get off the plane, get on a bus, get off

the bus, get herded into a hotel,
training, back on again to the ho
There's little opportunity to take
your own or with a couple of lik

Then there are the local bugs
I travelled to Western Samoa w
1990 and a bunch of us were lai
all got sick there again three years later, but that th
our own fault. We'd been warned not to drink the local water
and the Queensland Rugby Union even supplied us with
bottled water at a cost of $180 a day. But did we listen? We
did not. Those of us who got sick had partaken of cordial
when we visited a school in Apia, stupidly forgetting that a
glass of cordial is mostly made of water. Gosh, I was crook!
But Jason Little, who spent most of his time on the island
vomiting violently, and Garrick Morgan who shed 5 kilograms in a couple of days, did it even tougher. The bug still
had us in its grip a week later when we played below par for
our Super 10 match against Auckland.

The most interesting country I ever visited? That's very
hard to say. I liked Europe because of its history, but because
it's so cold you're forced to spend too much time indoors
where it's stuffy and smoky. New Zealand is truly beautiful
and I want to take my family there. I enjoyed South Africa
because it looks very much like Australia and, just like us,
it is a land of enormous potential. It's just unfortunate
that South Africa has been racked with turmoil for so many
years, and it will take a little time before its potential is
realised. South Africans take their rugby seriously, of course.
Sometimes *too* seriously. In all honesty, I didn't enjoy meeting some of the fans there because they truly believe they

best rugby team in the world and every other
tion is second rate. They are capable of unbelievable
ess and aggression to visitors.

South African fans are something different from your
average footy follower. Pretty much everywhere I've toured,
the public respects visiting players. Yes, they want us to lose
out on the field, but they make us welcome in their country.
Maybe they'll come on with a bit of friendly banter in a bar
– 'Look, mate, my name's such-and-such and I just wanted
to say bad luck about today,' or whatever – or ask for an
autograph. That's fine, and appreciated. But South African
fans would come up to us in a pub and get right in our faces.
Once one walked up to me and sneered, 'We're too strong
and too good for you Wallabies. Os du Randt beat your arse
today!' I replied, 'Mate, I'm not interested.' He came back at
me with more trash talk and I said, 'Rack off, mate. If you
can't talk sensibly to me, then scram.' Then he got all injured:
'Oh, don't get up *me*, Crowley. I'm only trying to have a joke.
Can't you Aussies *take* a little joke.' They think they're helping out their team by being rude to opponents. But I suppose
it's the same anywhere: it only takes a few idiots to give a
whole nation a bad name.

When I was a boy I travelled extensively throughout
Australia with my family and developed an early appreciation of how wonderful our country is. All the same, it's very
important for Australians to travel overseas, to see the rest of
the world and to lap up all the great things on offer to the
inquisitive visitor. But in spite of all the galleries and cathe-
drals and cuisines and cultures and landmarks, I believe one
of the big attractions of venturing overseas is that doing so
proves just how great life is in Australia. We've got it so good

here with our friendly people, wonderful beaches, our out-back and cities. The freedom, the peace.

Last year I took my children to Fiji, and we went to the local village and the kids' jaws just hit the ground when they saw how the locals lived: in shacks made of corrugated iron supported by four sticks in the ground and a trough of water. My daughter was like, 'Well, what's this?' And I told her, 'This is where they live, mate. This is what their life is about.' And she was like, 'Holey Moley!'

There are a lot of people in this country who want to whinge and carry on about how terrible it is here. Most of them have never left their backyard to see what it's like else-where. When I was in the police force in Nanango I met a fellow who was 22 and had never been to Brisbane because his father had never been. What chance has that poor guy got?

Back in 1990, after struggling off the field in the Western Samoa game, it took two weeks of intense physiotherapy before I recovered sufficiently to pack down with Cameron Lillicrap and Mark McBain in the Reds front row when we walloped the Soviet Union. Though still hampered, I then played in our helter-skelter win against the strong Kiwi side, Canterbury, in the South Pacific Cup. We started off strongly and hit a handy lead, then with the crowd behind them Canterbury came roaring back at us, throwing the ball around with abandon, as if they were playing sevens, trying to run us off our feet. Unprepared for this onslaught we were tearing all over the field to try to halt their progress. I found myself tackling wingers. At first these unorthodox tactics paid off and they almost caught us. Then we got a second wind and won handily 31–16.

When we faced NSW at Ballymore in late May, we were in the unusual position of having won our last three encounters. The forward planning of 1987, when Reds administrators began putting together a strong and committed state team to whom victory over NSW was an end in itself and not just a means of getting into the Australian side, was bearing fruit. This match, however, was an acid test. We knew NSW were smarting and pumped and we were determined to prove that we had the wood on the Blues after all those years of beatings. On a personal level, I was determined to get stuck into the NSW front row of McKenzie, Kearns and Tony Daly, by that time the incumbent Test 1, 2 and 3.

NSW had a wonderful side which included Farr-Jones, Tim Gavin, Simon Poidevin, Steve Cutler, Peter FitzSimons, who'd starred on the recent Wallaby tour of France, as well as the aforementioned front row who, as much as I wanted to punish them on the field, I acknowledged as a terrific trio. But we were no slouches either, with Paul Carozza, Horan and Little, Lynagh, Slattery, Scott-Young, Jeff Miller, David Wilson, Bill Campbell, Rod McCall, and McBain and Matt Ryan packing down with me upfront. Yes, we were smaller right across the park, but we were passionate Reds and figured that would compensate.

It did. We were gone for all money as the second-half began, down 8–3 and battling to stay in the game. Five metres out from our line, the vaunted NSW scrum attempted a pushover try, but we busted our guts, stood 'em up and pushed 'em back. That's all it took to turn the match around. Just like that, momentum swung our way. In the 46th minute, their five-eighth John Mulvihill rocketed a cut-out pass to his unmarked Fijian winger Acura Niuqila. It *was* a

Fijian winger who caught the ball on the fly. Problem was, it was *our* Fijian, Isei Siganiyavi, who'd come in-field and plucked the ball out of the air. He then ran 95 metres to score. Suddenly, we were ahead 9–8. We were unstoppable in the lineouts, rucks and mauls as well as the scrum, and at game's end we won 22–14. I was named Man of the Match, but still couldn't oust Ewen McKenzie from the Australian tight head spot for the three Test series against France in June and an international against the United States in July. Nor, also in July, could I even make the 30-man Wallaby team for New Zealand. McKenzie, Kearns and Daly, the blokes McBain, Ryan and I had shunted all over Ballymore in Queensland's interstate win, once more formed the front row for all three Tests in a series won 2–1 by the All Blacks.

David Wilson was an enormous asset to Queensland and Australia, and a bloke who had my total respect. He was mentally and physically tough, but he would never have a go at an opposition player unless he'd been provoked. He was, and remains, a great mate. Not that that helped him when he turned out for Easts in one grand final against Souths. Dave was their best player by far against us that day. In fact, he was all that stood between us and another premiership. He knew that with Tim Horan, Jason Little and Damian Smith in our backs we had more strike power than Easts, so he took it upon himself to slow the ball down and try to at least prevent a slaughter. We had five internationals in our pack, including enforcers Garrick Morgan, Troy Coker and Sam Scott-Young, and when we saw what Dave was up to, we got together and said, 'Well, he's a mate . . . but he's trying to kill the ball, slow it down and stop us from winning, so we have to deal with the problem by taking him out of the game.' So, we made Dave our target. He ended the game with a fractured cheekbone and a gash in his head that took 20 stitches to close. In one ruck we were giving it to him with such venom that our own winger, Damian Smith, ran in and abused us and told us to leave him alone.

We felt bad afterwards that we'd punished Dave. In fairness, we *had* warned him to stop trying to slow the ball down. He later told us, 'I just had to do it, and I had no doubt about what would be coming my way.' One thing about this crazy, testosterone-filled, brutal sport of rugby is that the main job of every player is to go out there and physically and mentally dominate the opposition. If it happens that a good mate is a member of that opposition, then so be it.

And speaking of blokes I respected, Sam Scott-Young has to be right up there. We didn't play much international footy together, but we were in many Queensland packs. It's an old cliché, but if there was a war, Sammy would be the guy I'd want in the trench beside me. While I'm handing out gongs, I've got to mention Richard Loe, Peter Clohessy, Guy Kebble, JJ Styger, Martin Johnson and Andrew Blades. Bladesy worked hard for a long time and put his body through a battering to become a top prop and once he made it he didn't stick around as a Wallaby for long, but I admired his work ethic. In my view he's the unsung hero of Australia's 1999 World Cup victory. Sean Fitzpatrick, the All Black skipper, was another interesting tough-nut. An inspirational leader and a terrific hooker. He was also a niggler, a fight-starter, a foot-twister, and probably the worst sledger the game has known. He was brutal, and he could also back up his words with muscle. We didn't get in each other's face. If he didn't think he could psych you out he'd leave you alone.

He terrorised Phil Kearns early on, till Phil fought back by scoring a try under Sean's nose then never letting him forget it. He tried to put John Eales off his game for a long time. Once again, off the field Fitzy's a good bloke. What happens on the field stays on the field.

And Tim Horan is a true champion. Sure, he was a skilful and dynamic centre, but what impressed me was the way he battled back from an horrific knee injury to reclaim his place as the best centre in the game and be named the best player in the 1999 World Cup. How many blokes do you hear moaning that if only it hadn't been for injury they would have been a top-liner? When a *true* top-liner gets injured he doesn't waste his days whining. He knuckles down and does whatever it takes to play again.

Making the Emerging Wallabies side that toured Europe in 1990 was adequate, if not total, compensation for being on the outer with the Test selectors. We won six matches, drew one and lost one, but that tour will be remembered most for the emergence of Queensland rookie forward John Eales, about whom coach Bob Hitchcock said, 'Eales is one of the most talented footballers I have ever seen. He has beautiful hands, runs powerfully with the ball and is one of those truly great players who can reach the top without any nastiness in his game.' (I lacked most of John's skills, and maybe I tried to compensate for that with aggression.)

The NSW front row trio held their positions in 15 of the 16 Tests that Australia played between July 1991 and August 1992. I managed to squeeze in a World Cup match when we beat Western Samoa 9–6 in Pontypool, Wales, October '91, but watched the big games from the sideline. I admit to entertaining mixed feelings when Nick Farr-Jones' side beat England in the World Cup final at Twickenham. Yes, I was delighted for the boys and it was an honour to be in the squad, but I believed I should have been out there on the field fighting the fight for my country. Of course, the convention is that everyone in the squad contributes to the victory no matter whether they played or not. But I don't buy that. The victory *truly* belongs to the boys who went out onto the field and won.

Oh yes, and on that great day I also proved I didn't give a XXXX for propriety when I presented Queen Elizabeth with a Fourex-branded football as she was introduced to both teams before the kick-off. It was just a show of colonial irreverence – the Queen and commercialism go together about as well as her prize corgi and an alley cat. Fourex was our sponsor and they'd been good to us, giving us T-shirts and other goods that we could raffle to raise money for the team fund. So, whenever we could, we went out of our way to get the Fourex name noticed. I recall Chris Handy was in strife because when he was doing the TV call, which was sponsored by Heineken beer, he defied orders and insisted on calling us the Fourex Wallabies. He was going to be rewarded by Fourex if he mentioned them, and he kept it up even after the international broadcaster threatened to pull the plug on the broadcast if he persisted.

Well, before the World Cup final at Twickenham, we reserves were supposed to kick the Fourex balls into the crowd and I came up with a plan. 'Hey, wouldn't it be a scream if we gave a Fourex ball to the Queen? The corgis could kick it around at the palace.' I was mucking around, but Nick Farr-Jones overheard me. Once more, my smart mouth had got me into trouble. 'I dare you to,' said Nick. 'You wouldn't be game.' I replied, 'I would!' He said, 'Mate, you're on!' When the Queen moved down our line she came to me and stopped and wished me good luck. 'Thank you, Ma'am,' I said, 'and here's one of our footballs as a token of our appreciation.' And I gave her the yellow ball, which resembled a piece of mozzarella cheese, with the Fourex logo plastered all over it. 'Oh, thank you very much,' she replied, looked at it, and moved on. I was afraid I was going to get jumped by MI5.

I reckoned at first that the Queen would have gone back to her royal box muttering, 'Insolent little colonial!', but I have it on good authority that she didn't mind the joke in the slightest and that the corgis have been kicking the cover off the ball ever since.

Another fine memory of the '91 World Cup was a dinner every player from every country was invited to in a huge hall. Up on the stage, separated from the players, was the longest table I had ever seen at which were sitting all the International Rugby Board blokes, all 52 or so of them. The players were crammed together down on the floor. It was a real us and them situation. At my table was Phil Kearns and Will Carling, the English skipper. We decided to make the best of the situation by having some fun with a drinking game. It was one of those contests where you have to memorise and recite, and if you mess up you have to skol a glass of wine. Carling was brilliant. Right in the middle of his turn, even while totally smashed, he had to stand up and make a speech to the esteemed gathering. Will didn't miss a beat. As he was saying, 'Thank you to the IRB on behalf of all the players for staging this marvellous event . . . ' he would blurt out his part in the game . . . something about a raving cockatoo. It was surreal. A remarkable performance, and somehow he made it sound like part of his speech.

I vowed to train hard in the off-season and make 1992 a winner, but, realistically, I had no reason to think my day would ever come . . .

Funny thing, I almost didn't even qualify for the '91 World Cup team. My hamstring tear made me miss Queensland's games against the visiting England and Wales sides. Still, in spite of my inactivity, I was picked in the touring squad. But then, at the 11th hour, after the Wallaby side was named, came another disaster when I was sent off for trampling the shoulder of Easts' Shaun Hourigan in the preliminary final of the club competition. It was a fair cop. For a while I looked certain to be suspended and it seemed certain that I'd have to forfeit my spot in the World Cup side. Happily, the judiciary took pity on me and let me tour. I don't know if Shaun, who was left nursing a badly grazed shoulder, shared in the rejoicing at my good fortune. Not that the judiciary let me off scot-free. They rubbed me out of the grand final (which really hurt because Souths won), the Australian club championship final and the pre-season trials and the opening matches of the 1992 season, a total of eight games. I didn't whinge. You do the crime . . .

A typically slushy Waikato day in May '92 turned out to be a red-letter one for me. I scored a try. Queensland were playing the locals and we reefed the ball high to their stand-in fullback, Eugene Martin. He dropped it, and I hared in, picked the ball up out of the mud one-handed and outpaced the cover defence to score, so doubling my try tally from

46 matches for my state. I was mildly shocked when coach Connolly named me as tight head for the following week's match, against the old enemy, NSW. I was half expecting to be picked on the wing.

The Queensland–NSW match, at Sydney's Waratah Park, would decide the winner of that year's Super Six tournament, an early and cut-down version of today's Super 12 series. We won that game 23–18. Connolly said it was as intense as any Test match and I won't disagree. All our games against NSW were fierce struggles. We got on with the New South Welshmen when we joined them in the Australian side, but we were deadly enemies in interstate clashes. As usual, it was fierce upfront with Tommy Lawton, Cameron Lillicrap and me tearing into McKenzie, Kearns and Daly and them returning the favour. I reckon we had a clear points victory that day. John Eales, Sam Scott-Young and David Wilson were magnificent in the win that gave us the right to call ourselves the best provincial side in the world.

In July, for my 50th game for Queensland, I lined up with Cameron and Tommy to oppose another red-hot front row, the All Blacks' Steve McDowell, Sean Fitzpatrick and Olo Brown. New Zealand beat us 26–19, but our forwards bested theirs. I took an injured calf muscle into the game, but carried on, feeling no pain – well, not much, anyway – as we took the mighty All Blacks right to the wire.

That calf injury kept me out of football for nearly three months, eliminating me from contention for Tests against New Zealand and a Wallaby trip to South Africa. My comeback match was in the grand final in September, when Souths played a strong University team. I was desperate to play, not just to help notch another premiership victory for the Magpies, but to grab a spot on the Wallaby tour of Ireland and Wales that would follow the domestic season.

The '92 grand final was as satisfying a club match as I ever played, right up there with our landmark '86 win. The cream of Queensland football ran onto Ballymore that day. Our team boasted Jason Little, Tim Horan, Damian Smith, Garrick Morgan, Sam Scott-Young, Troy Coker, Adrian Skeggs, Mark Connors, our skipper Fraser Perrin and, playing his last match, Tom Lawton. Lining up for the Students were Wallabies Greg Martin, Michael Lynagh, Cameron Lillicrap, David Nucifora and Peter Slattery.

University asked a lot of questions of us early, as we knew they would, then our huge and powerful pack gained control with rock-solid scrums and aggressive rucking and mauling topped off with damaging charges from Coker, Scott-Young and, especially, Morgan, who I remember sat Slats fair on his backside when the tough Uni halfback had tried to take him head-on. As Tommy Lawton said later, 'We let the dogs loose!' Two of our tries, to Coker and Lawton, came from rolling mauls after Morgan had won clean ball. Connors' try resulted from us pushing their pack back over their own try-line. We won the second-half lineouts 12–2. Ascendancy established, we then unleashed the backs. The 44–10 final scoreline, seven tries to one, was the widest grand final margin ever in Brisbane club football. As well as first grade, we won seconds, thirds and fourths and so wrapped up the club championship two years running.

These days, with the super-heavy representative workload imposed on rugby's elite players by Super 12 and Wallaby commitments, it's rare for stars to turn out for their club side.

But back in 1992, Souths were able to field our best available side, and in so doing vied with the great Randwick teams of old as the strongest club line-up ever to run on to an Australian rugby field. 'We have come from a time when the club could not win more than two games a year,' declared a euphoric coach Phil White, 'and now we want to keep this club going.' We went on to win another four or five premierships in my time.

The Wallaby team was named the day after the grand final. We expected good representation and we weren't disappointed. Souths men Damian Smith, Little and Horan, Scott-Young, Coker, Morgan and myself made the team, which was heavy with Queenslanders, and, after the thrashings we dealt to NSW that year, rightly so. I was back in the green-and-gold jersey and determined that my wilderness years were over at last.

What a tour, rich in wonderful performances and incidents we'll never forget. It was great to be a Wallaby again, and, my usual homesickness aside, I had a ball on and off the field. There is an old Wallaby tradition that each of the players has to serve a stint as duty boy, that is, making sure the day runs to schedule and being a dogsbody for the other guys. I relished the role. I didn't even mind bowing and scraping to the blokes from NSW. Well, not much. Tim Horan and I, who've been mates since early days at Souths, were joint duty boys the day we left Dublin and travelled to Cork for our match against Munster. The duty boy's job is to ensure the balls are all there, and there's plenty of water. But Tim and I took our responsibilities much more seriously than that. Both of us dressed in slacks, jacket, white shirt and bow tie, then knocked on each of the guys' hotel doors to wake them up and offer them a newspaper and a glass of orange juice. Then we told them when they'd have to be down in the breakfast room and took their breakfast order so their food could all be waiting for them. While they were eating, we lugged all their bags onto the bus along with any fruit, sweets, drinks and R-rated videos that they might have ordered . . . We helped them board the bus and even escorted coach Bob Dwyer to his seat. During the trip we attended to every player's whims, doled out more newspapers and lollies, generally spread good cheer, and at the end of the four-hour journey woke each guy gently. We'd also organised that drinks be served when the team disembarked at Cork. The guys loved it.

I was picked on the bench for the early tour game against Leinster but got onto the paddock, as loose-head prop, in the 21st minute when Tony Daly was injured. I gave it everything. Reported Greg Growden of the *Sydney Morning Herald*, 'Crowley showed all the passion of a person striving for a Test position. He was feverishly fearless, doing all that was required of a person wanting to take an injured man's Test spot.' Prophetic words, for when Tony was ruled out of the Test against Ireland I got his position and played my first international as a loose head.

The game before the one-off Ireland Test pitted us against the ferocious and committed Munster team, a side which over the years had routinely beaten touring sides and which fielded six internationals including Peter Clohessy, a stocky, balding bloke who preferred a fight to a feed any day of the week. A brawl was always going to happen. Clohessy got me a good one. He stomped on the back of my head in the opening minutes and opened me right up. It was a cold day and it hurt like hell. My head was dripping blood. Anthony Herbert, trying, I guess, to make me feel better, came over and said, 'It's only a scratch, mate. You'll be right.' All the boys were killing themselves laughing. The medic put 22 stitches in my deeply gashed head. Then I picked myself up and tore back into the fray, only to be dismissed by the referee for excessive bleeding.

Next day my head was wrapped up like a mummy, and it hurt for weeks. I sported the world's biggest zipper, and to this day I still have a warp in my melon. (After the match, Munster's coach refused to condemn Clohessy, who was involved in most of the unsavoury incidents and once king-hit Ewen McKenzie in back play. 'I don't know what all the fuss is about. Peter did what he was picked to do. He played very well.') For all his sins, Cloey is a good bloke, and he and I buried the hatchet over a number of beers after the game.

Peter and I were by no means the only ones mixing brawling with football. At one stage 20 guys were going at each other hammer and tongs. Punching, kicking and grappling. Garrick Morgan and their Mick Galway were sent off on the charge of 'wrestling on the ground'. Later, Garrick insisted he was only trying to keep Galway and his cohorts from murdering Ewen McKenzie. Bob Dwyer, too, stuck up for his men. 'Contrary to the laws of rugby, I think that if you're attacked you're entitled to defend yourself.'

If Munster's ploy was to put us off our game, they succeeded. We were woeful, repeatedly turning the ball over at breakdowns and in the lineout, and scrummaging poorly. Each side scored a try, but they kicked more goals and downed us 22–19.

Next day at our hotel before we trained, coach Bob Dwyer tore into us. He really went berserk, singling out each player in turn for abuse. He got up every bloke, and when he finally came to me I was expecting the worst. But he left me alone. I reckon he took one look at my battered head and reckoned I'd suffered enough.

The fellows who hadn't played in the match could hear Bob's screaming through the walls. They actually ran past the door on their way from physiotherapy, terrified that he'd come out and see them and accuse them of eavesdropping. Bob was a hard man, but a brilliant coach. The only problem was that many of his advanced ideas on how to play the game were too complex for the players. In the end, it was like all coaches. If they pick you in their team you love 'em. If they don't, they're hopeless.

For our next match against Ulster, scheduled just three days after the Munster donnybrook, I was on the bench but blokes were dropping like flies and they had no one else by that stage of the tour. All the boys were taking potshots at me, saying, 'Hey, Crowls, I hope you get on the field,' and tapping me on the head where the wound was. I snapped back, 'There's *no way* they're getting me out onto that field!' Then, 30 minutes into the game, Lillicrap got into a fight and broke his thumb. To his credit he stayed on until half-time. Guess who replaced him, after they stuck four painkillers around my wound. I lasted only a couple of minutes before my stitches started to split. After the game the doctor stitched me up again. No real harm done.

It didn't take a brain surgeon to tell us that Ireland would follow Munster's lead and try to belt us out of the Test match. I was chosen out of position at loose head when

Tony Daly hurt his back and was sent home, and of course Lillicrap had broken his thumb. I was the last man standing. In the lead-up to the big Lansdowne Road match, all the talk was of an impending roughhouse. 'After what happened at Munster they'll think we can be unsettled if they turn it on,' Michael Lynagh told reporters. 'If I was the Irish coach I would see this as a weakness for his team to exploit. Still, I would like them to try it. We have a very tough and aggressive forward pack.' He had a point, for our forward line-up comprised Kearns, McKenzie, McCall and Eales, Wilson, Willie Ofahengaue, and Tim Gavin. Our backs, which included Campese, Carozza, Little, Horan, and Lynagh, weren't bad either.

In the end, as often happens when a blue is predicted, the game was tame. We dominated possession and the Irish were too busy trying to catch Campese and Co to fight. We thrashed them 42–17, five tries to one.

With Lillicrap and Daly injured and out of the tour, they had flown in my Reds' teammate Matt Ryan as a replacement for the Test. I copped another four painkillers before the game and I remember thinking, 'Holy hell! The fun's gone right of this tour.' Twenty minutes into the Test we put on a lineout move, and I grabbed the ball and ran down the sideline and got tackled. Tim Gavin raced in and kicked at the ball but collected my chin with his boot. Result: another huge and bloody gash right through to the jawbone. I was in for another stitching. Twenty this time. In those pre-blood-bin days I had to go off the field, get stitched up, and be back on within three minutes or I was out of the game. Bob Dwyer didn't want to use Matt Ryan because he was still jetlagged from the long trip from Australia, and he demanded that the doctor do his work quickly. So there was no time for an anaesthetic. 'Crowls, this is going to hurt,' said the doc, a bit unnecessarily. In went the stitches to hold my gaping face together and I ran back onto the field with 10 seconds to go. Matt was bitterly disappointed that he didn't get onto the paddock. After that day, he never again had the opportunity to play for Australia in a Test. I suspect that deep down in his heart, he'll never forgive me!

Upon my return to the field I lined up for a lineout facing my opposite, Peter Clohessy. He took one look at me and said, 'Fookin' 'ell, what a mess! You won't be kissin' my sister tonight with a face like that!' and on with the game.

Next up, Wales, and with Daly back in Australia, I got picked for that Test too. Two Tests in a row. I was on a roll. And when we won easily, 23–6, it was clear the Wallabies were too. The Welshmen gave it to us in the first-half, and led 3–0 just before the break. Then our fullback, Marty Roebuck, took a penalty shot from in front. The ball hit the upright and bounced back into the field of play, right into Roebuck's arms. Our breakaway, David Wilson, recalled what happened next: 'Marty fed it to Phil Kearns. As soon as we saw that, we lifted a gear, all the forwards just piled in and there was a drive right to their line. Crowls gave it to Garrick, and Garrick and I just rolled. He sort of shielded me. I just kept low and burrowed over from a metre out.' That was the turning point of the match and we crossed twice more in the second-half for a very sweet victory.

Our final major international on that tour was at Twickenham against the Barbarians, a team made up of play-ers from different countries who traditionally throw the ball around in a bid to entertain the fans. We decided not to play that style of game on this occasion, and treated the match as a Test that we had no intention of losing. We played it tight, refusing to be drawn into the Barbarians' cavalier style. The fans who'd turned up hungry for razzle-dazzle were not amused by our conservative, safety first, approach. I have a feeling, however, that true rugby aficionados would have been delighted by the tries Phil Kearns and I scored as a result of textbook rolling mauls. Even during a game, the potshots don't stop. I recall that after scoring a try, I was walking back to halfway with Troy Coker. Never one to let a chance go by, Troy pointed to my name on the scoreboard as the try scorer. 'Have a good look there, Crowls – good chance you'll never see it again.' Our 30–20 win wrapped up the campaign.

At tour's end, coach Bob Dwyer rated his players to a Sydney journalist, which a number of the boys were furious about. The top performers got an A Plus, the next best were given an A, B Plus, B, C Plus and those who hadn't measured up received a C. Among the elite were Campese, Eales, Gavin, Horan, Kearns, Little, Lynagh, McCall, McKenzie, Ofahengaue, Wilson . . . and Crowley.

It seemed Bob Dwyer was a fan at last. And, as the 1993 season began, I reckoned that my recent good form at rugby's highest level would nail down a regular spot in the Test team, either as a tight-head or loose-head prop. Things didn't work out that way. Most of the year I was hampered by an excruciating hernia I picked up in a game for Queensland against Fiji, then destroyed it – or, should I say, Guy Kebble destroyed it – against Natal. The injury, and damaged ribs, kept me sidelined for much of the season and doomed me to sit by helplessly as a fit-again Tony Daly waltzed back into his regular position in the engine room of the Wallaby scrum. Daly was a good player. When he first started and was trying to make the Wallabies in the early 1990s he was very good indeed. Then, when he became a fixture in the team I don't believe he put as much into his game and he faded from the international scene about 1996.

I did make it back in time for the grand final, but in that match I damaged a knee cartilage which put me under a cloud for the Wallaby tour of the United States, Canada and France. Somehow I got picked, but the closest I came to making the Tests was a run as a replacement for Daly in the Test against Canada in Calgary. We won 43–16, but it was a scrappy, lack-lustre affair in which no one distinguished himself.

I was busting to get onto the field against the French in Paris, but it wasn't to be. We lost the First Test 16–13 after blowing a number of scoring chances. I thought I had a chance of unseating McKenzie or Daly for the Second and final Test but coach Bob Dwyer stayed loyal to the pair who, in fairness, had done everything asked of them and more in the First Test loss. As it happened, we turned the tables in the Second Test and won 24–3 in spite of the French resorting to eye gouging and testicle grabbing. When we returned home I booked myself in for an operation to repair my hernia, which was still giving me hell.

I'm a philosophical kind of bloke. I believe that in life, and in rugby, we get a pretty equal share of good and bad luck. But I reckoned the football fates were conspiring against me when injuries damn-near crippled my season in 1994. In

February, my stomach still had not recovered and I missed out on Queensland's tour of Argentina. Facing the behemoths of the Pampas with a hernia is not recommended. Then, in April, playing in the Reds' 24–18 Super 10 series loss to Otago I again suffered a serious calf injury that bundled me out for the next five weeks.

I consoled myself that I was in better shape than Tim Horan. My old duty-boy buddy suffered a shocking knee injury against Natal. By tearing his anterior cruciate ligament, both cartilages, and dislocating his kneecap he booked himself in for a major knee reconstruction.

The only consolation for a season in which I missed out on playing Tests against Ireland, Italy, Western Samoa and New Zealand, as well as for Queensland in most of the Super 10 matches and a swag of games for Souths was that I was picked at age 28 in, wait for it, the Emerging Wallabies side to play some matches in Africa. This team, which selectors get together on an irregular basis, is not quite accurately named. The idea is that a bunch of promising young players who may one day be Wallabies embark on an overseas tour under the guidance of an experienced captain and a handful of senior players. I was named skipper for that '94 tour, and in my care were some special young guys who found their feet and went on to do the Wallabies proud. I'm talking about Joe Roff, Daniel Herbert, Owen Finegan, Andrew Blades and Richard Harry.

I may not have been the best player ever to turn out for Australia, but I reckon I was one of the most persistent. By the time I was 29, as season 1995 got underway, I'd been considered one of the three or four best props in the land, but in the six years since I'd made my debut against the

British Lions in July 1989, I'd played just six more Tests. Due to the repeated selection of Ewen McKenzie and Tony Daly I'd never been able to crack it for a regular position in the Australian Test team. But I'd continued to give my all for my club, state (in fact, some say that playing for Queensland meant as much to me as playing for Australia), and whenever I got called up into the Test front row. I gave my all when my team was winning, and also when we were losing. When we were crunching the opposing pack, and when we were being crunched. I gave everything when I was fit or playing hurt. I never spat the dummy and criticised the selectors for not picking me. (Well, not to their faces, anyway.) I never sounded out the Brisbane Broncos league team about switching codes (not that I was going to be a prized league recruit). I soldiered on, hoping my day would come.

And it did, in 1995.

In 1995 and 1996, Australia played 19 Test matches, and I took the field in 12 of them, missing out on the outstanding seven largely because they were minor World Cup games and I was being rested, or through suspension. The reason I became a regular Wallaby at last was a combination of my finding a purple patch of form (possibly because I was enjoying my new role as a loose-head prop and, for the first time in three seasons, I was relatively injury-free) and Tony Daly suffering a form slump.

The warning bells had been ringing for Tony. I make a point of not reading the press all that much (if you lap it up when the journos praise you, then you also have to cop it on the chin when they bag you). But I read with interest a report by Andrew Dawson that was published in the Brisbane

Courier-Mail on 20 April 1995, just before the Test team to play the Pumas was picked:

> *Test rugby union prop Tony Daly is one of several Wallabies 'put on notice' as the selectors ponder the side to play Argentina on April 30. Form Queensland prop Dan Crowley has stormed into contention at a time when the national selectors have not been satisfied with Daly's performance. Daly, capped 39 times, will return from injury in second grade for Randwick this weekend.*
>
> *Chairman of selectors Paul McLean stressed Daly had not been singled out by the panel; several other World Cup players had been told they were not performing to their ability. 'We have had a few chats with Tony over the past fortnight, but we have also chatted to a few other players and put them on notice,' McLean said. 'Tony is not the only player in that category. They might think they are playing well, but we know they can do better.'*
>
> *Crowley's form over the Super 10 Series was enough to warrant consideration for Test selection, but Daly's plight has intensified his claims. It would be a tough decision by the selectors to split the record-breaking front three of Daly, Phil Kearns and Ewen Mckenzie, so well have they served Australia over the years. But Crowley, 29, has never played better than this season. Capable of playing both sides of the scrum during a distinguished 72-match career with Queensland, the mobile and skilful Crowley played loose head prop for Australia as a replacement for the injured Daly on the 1992 tour of Wales and Ireland and provides an all-round option for the panel seeking more than scrummaging prowess.*

Three days later when I learnt of the team chosen to play Argentina, after years as a back-up for Tony Daly I discovered that I had finally prised the New South Welshman from the Wallaby front row. McKenzie, Kearns, Crowley – it had a sweet ring.

We put the Pumas to the sword 53–7 in Brisbane and 30–13 in Sydney, but the second match was a real Test. With their trademark strong forward pack giving as much, sometimes more, than they got, Argentina led us 13–3 at halftime. After the break our forwards went up a gear and we were able to dominate, and the score blew out in the dying minutes.

Any Test win is to be savoured, but no one was fooled. With the 1995 World Cup in South Africa just weeks away, we had problems. It wasn't that the Wallabies didn't have a strong squad capable of defending the Cup we'd won at Twickenham four years earlier. Any team with Eales, Campese, Lynagh, Little, Gavin, Wilson, Ofahengaue, McCall, Kearns and McKenzie, and Wallaby legends-to-be George Gregan, Joe Roff and Matt Burke, is not going to be a pushover. But when push came to shove, we were disappointing. Our wins, against Canada (27–11) and Romania (42–3) were unconvincing. Against Canada, we were truly appalling. We scored 17 points fast, then bumbled and fumbled for the rest of the game. And we were rolled by the eventual World Cup winners, South Africa (27–18), in a pool match and by England (25–22) in Capetown, courtesy of a classic Rob Andrew field goal, in the quarter-final.

Right on fulltime we were locked on 22–all, two tries apiece, then Andrew coolly slotted the goal (a portent of another decisive and heartbreaking field goal that would be booted by another Englishman, named Wilkinson, in

Sydney eight years later). That match was Michael Lynagh's last Test. Ours was an unceremonious exit from the 1995 World Cup, and not even the wonderful sight of South African President Nelson Mandela celebrating in a Springbok jersey could lift our spirits.

New Zealand were unlucky not to win the World Cup. They played well throughout the series but were victims of a South African side who, because they were on an emotional high and enjoyed the hysterical support of their fans, were always going to be hard to beat if they made the final. The All Blacks' giant winger Jonah Lomu was the player of the tournament, and his four-try tour de force against England in the semi-final was one of the great performances by a player in the history of rugby. He was literally unstoppable, and it's a tragedy that chronic illness prevented him from ever being quite so good again, although he came real close against us a few weeks later.

I believe our 1995 campaign came unstuck because we weren't as mentally prepared as we should have been. We thought we were better than we really were, and were simply not equipped in that early pool game to take on the Springboks, who would have died for their country that day. They hit us with everything and we buckled. If we'd managed to beat England in the quarter-final, I'm pretty sure the All Blacks would have rolled us the week after, maybe not as comprehensively as New Zealand beat England, as we know how to play the Blacks better than the Poms do because we play them more often, but they would have downed us just the same.

Jonah Lomu was one of the lethal weapons we knew we'd have to defuse to have a chance when we played the first of our two Bledisloe Cup Tests against the All Blacks in Auckland in July. He wasn't the only danger man either. Throw in the ace centre pairing of Frank Bunce and Walter Little, five-eighth Andrew Mehrtens, and a killer pack comprising the Brooke brothers Zinzan and Robin, Josh Kronfeld, Mike Brewer, Ian Jones, Olo Brown, Sean Fitzpatrick and Craig Dowd, one of the all-time great packs, and you'll understand why we weren't exactly favourites. This was especially the case since we were taking them on without Lynagh (retired) and Campese (dropped). They won 28–16 and it was a typical bloody All Black–Australia slugfest. One try each, and they got home on Mehrtens' boot in the last quarter of the game.

It was as hard upfront as you'd expect, with no quarter given and certainly none asked. I saw Josh Kronfeld on the ground and I stomped on him. I thought nothing much more of it, and I suspect Josh didn't either – he was near the ball. But the video ref did. I was cited on video evidence and suspended for three weeks, the first player ever to suffer this fate.

Some people in the media, and certainly the New Zealand press, got stuck into me but, hey, any good prop walks a fine line between controlled aggression and going over the top. My longtime Queensland coach, John Connolly, came out in support of me: 'Dan has been the cornerstone of some of our great wins over France and England and in the Super 10s Series finals. He has been a very influential person within the group.' And Queensland hooker Michael Foley weighed in: 'He thrives on pressure situations, plays his best when others struggle in really tough situations.'

Mark Harthill took my place for the next Test, in Sydney.

We had Jonah Lomu's measure in Auckland but in Sydney we got a taste of what England experienced. Of the All Blacks' five tries, Lomu scored one, set up three and handled in another. After the game, won 34–23 by the Blacks, Bob Dwyer, who was coaching Australia for the last time, sighed, 'I don't think there's ever been another one like Lomu.'

Another to speak after that Test was our skipper Phil Kearns, who declared to the fans, 'We hope whatever happens in the future, you'll continue to support us.' To most who heard him, these were seemingly innocuous words. But their full import became crystal clear in the days and weeks ahead.

9

REVOLUTION
IN THE AIR

As the 1995 season began, Australian rugby had long ceased to be an amateur game. Yes, no one was supposed to be paid for playing, but certain high-profile players were making five-figure sums a year when travel allowances, off-field obligations and product endorsements were added together. Fair enough, too. But, after rumblings of discontent from players for the past few years that they were being poorly paid for their skills and effort, '95 was the year when rugby went fully professional and elite players' salaries soared into the stratosphere. Rupert Murdoch's Super League's attempt to hijack rugby league from the Australian Rugby League kicked off in 1995, and was the catalyst for a new era. League clubs, notably the cashed up and professionally run Brisbane Broncos, who were a major proponent of Super League, hungrily sought to poach the cream of rugby's crop. To keep them at bay, rugby union officials opened their coffers.

Just before the World Cup final between the Springboks and the All Blacks was staged in South Africa in June, the Australian, South African and New Zealand rugby unions broke the news that they had signed a $US550 million 10-year TV rights deal with Murdoch's international organisation News Corporation. What Murdoch's viewers would be watching were two new competitions: the Super 12s, in which 12 state and provincial teams from the three nations (the Queensland Reds, the NSW Waratahs and a new team, the ACT Brumbies, represented Australia) would do battle in a round-robin tournament each year; and an annual triangular Test series contested by Australia, New Zealand and South Africa, which would incorporate the existing Bledisloe Cup clashes between Australia and New Zealand. The deal would also provide top players with annual six-figure salaries.

It's not hard to see why the News Corporation scheme had such appeal for the game's administrators. Instead of a sprinkling of Test matches and a couple of interstate matches that often were not even televised, rugby's profile would be raised immeasurably with top-level matches on TV practically every week.

The Murdoch plan looked a done deal, until two months later a rebel group, the World Rugby Corporation, reared its head. The WRC, brainchild of sports journalist David Lord, and fronted by former Wallaby and businessman Ross Turnbull, declared that they would be abandoning establishment rugby and setting up a global structure for the game, à la Kerry Packer's World Series Cricket, with each country's national union sharing in the spoils. Turnbull announced that player payments would be more lucrative than those offered by the Murdoch plan and that the best players in the world, who had been contacted and courted by the rebels months before, and who included Australian captain Phil Kearns, were signing on the dotted line.

For a while, either side could have prevailed as the Dutch auction for the players' hearts, minds and pockets raged; then, as that turbulent season ended, Murdoch and the establishment trumped their rivals by offering targeted players literally millions of dollars via two- and three-year contracts to play Super 12s and for the national team. Unable to compete with this flood of cash, WRC folded, and those guys who'd thrown in their lot with the rebels jumped ship and were welcomed back into the establishment fold almost as if the whole bitter business had never happened.

In quick time, the International Rugby Board followed the Southern Hemisphere bodies' lead and the administrators in every rugby-playing nation, and their players and the players' lawyers and managers, were devising lucrative contracts that would buy the players homes, cars and race-horses; pay for school fees and help set them up for life. I was offered a great deal for three years. Six months before, the only time I'd have thought of reaping that kind of money would have been in terms of a Lotto win. I wasn't at the top of the heap, but I was very happy with my lot. Peter Jenkins reported in his comprehensive book, *Wallaby Gold: The History of Australian Test Rugby*, that fellows such as John Eales, the new Wallaby captain, and Jason Little were earning $450,000 and $500,000 a year respectively.

The players' riches came at a price, there being no such thing as a free lunch. On the agenda now for the elite were 11 Super 12 matches a year, or more if you made the finals, as well as at least 11 Tests in a World Cup year. In the world of professional rugby, a season would now stretch for at least eight months, travel would be constant, and family life become a distant memory. So too, it turned out, would playing club rugby. At the time, Peter Jenkins quoted Australian Rugby Union general manager John O'Neill as saying: 'These are professional players now. But we are aware of the fine balancing act that needs to be made, and the dangers of burnout. We don't want to overload the players. But, by the same token, television money pays their salaries and television wants product.'

Only 18 months before, I had severed my ties with the police and was now working hard in my new career, establishing a private investigation business. I thought I might as well stick to what I knew. But with the new and second pay packet came more responsibility. I was stuck with one foot in the past as an amateur holding down a job and another in the present as a professional rugby player. I knew I needed to keep a balance and another job because you are only ever one injury away from sitting on the sideline.

Being nouveau riche definitely went to a couple of blokes' heads. Not John Eales's nor Jason Little's, who are excellent blokes, I hasten to add. I tried not to allow either the extra money that was coming in or my contractual obligations to get in the way of my involvement with Souths. If I couldn't play with the boys as often as I wanted, I made sure I was part of the furniture of the club every chance I got. With our representative players unavailable to play and provide an example to the young blokes coming through the grades, I made a point of attending functions at Chipsy Wood Oval and often sat on the sideline during matches. I attended junior sign-on days and encouraged the guys as best I could. Rugby can't survive if it is only supported at the highest levels. Without healthy grassroots in the cities, towns and in the bush, our code has no future.

When in 1996 the Queensland Rugby Union proposed the establishment the following year of a televised national 10- or 12-team club competition with all the representative players obligated to take part to get the neglected clubs back into the limelight I backed them to the hilt. The idea was for the Australian Rugby Football Union to grant $50,000 to each of the competing clubs and recoup their money through pay TV broadcast rights and sponsorship. The idea, like many since, has fallen onto barren ground. Today the club competition still struggles.

Yes, the money nowadays is great and, I believe, extremely well deserved. A player only has a short life on the field and he has to make the most of it. While others are climbing the corporate ladder and going to university, we're playing footy, and when we retire we're in our early 30s and right behind the eight ball as far as providing for ourselves and our families is concerned.

But, that said, I reckon that rugby was more enjoyable in the old days, when it was just a game and not a business. I made more friends in the early part of my career than I did in the latter stages, post-professionalism. I think I know why. Back then, before sponsorship responsibilities, codes of conduct, dietitians, training camps and video analysis, we could empty the Esky of beer that was always waiting for us after a game, then we'd get stuck into the chicken wings, sausage rolls and party pies, and then we'd drink more beer. We had *fun*. And great friendships that I cherish to this day were forged. This is not denigrating any of the many terrific mates I've made since turning professional. Maybe it's just that the first friends you make are the staunchest.

Nor am I alone in having these thoughts. Rod McCall, another who straddled the two eras, expresses the same sentiment: 'It's a different culture since professionalism. Some younger blokes have never played a rugby game without collecting money. Take Dan Herbert, the former Queensland and Wallaby centre. Dan came into the Queensland team as a 19-year-old and was the first guy I knew who never had to work. He was just a professional rugby player. In the amateur days, obviously we all had to have jobs.

'My last year was the first year of professionalism, and I started noticing a change. Blokes were a lot less forgiving of a teammate who made a mistake on the field and cost them the game and therefore money. A different culture emerged. There was a new emphasis on results. It wasn't so much you were playing for your state, but for the money. It became more cut-throat. The fabric of the game changed. When professionalism came in, I saw some unhappy characteristics in blokes I thought I knew. It was a look-after-yourself-first philosophy.

'I can remember blokes like Crowls, and certainly myself, getting so many pain-killing needles and being patched up just to get on the paddock for Queensland because we were playing for pride. Nowadays, guys are less likely to play injured because a below-par performance could see them dropped from the side and that would cost them money. Every young bloke who comes in now has managers and all they're trying to do is set up their career and their bank balance.

'Professionalism was inevitable. It had to come, and for very good reasons. Unfortunately, it has bred greed. I reckon there wouldn't be five players out of a hundred or so con-tracted in Australia at this time who think they're being paid what they're worth. They're always saying, "I want more." Look, I know footballers have a limited time when they can set themselves up but a money-hungry attitude has had a bad impact on the culture of rugby.

'Gone now is the camaraderie. There just isn't the oppor-tunity any more with sponsors' obligations and daily training and measuring of performance. Playing for Queensland and the Wallabies, we'd get drunk once a week. And I *mean* drunk. Then we'd sober up, train hard and play the next week. It wasn't seen as detrimental then. It was just some-thing you did. If you toured and weren't in the Test side, you'd probably write yourself off twice a week.'

'Those late nights in bars and the moments we shared on tour helped to bind us and strengthen our friendships. We were able to find out what each of us was really like, what our dreams were. What we thought. When you're playing football you'll try harder for a bloke you respect and like. He'll tap you on the arse and say, "We need a big effort," and no matter how bad you're feeling, you'll put one foot in front of the other and do it for him.'

I agree with at least some of what Rod says.

10

BLEEDING RED

IT MEANT SO MUCH to me to play for Queensland. I never got blasé about hearing my name read out to play for the Reds. When, late in my career, I was named in Queensland's Team of the Century it was a tremendous honour, even though I'm not sure how the judges are able to choose between players from different eras. It's a hard one. Being selected in the Top 100 Years of Reds is something I'll appreciate more and more as the years go on. But when I was playing I couldn't give much thought to posterity. Sure, as a kid I looked up to the gun Queenslanders of their era, blokes like Tony Shaw, Mark Loane and Paul McLean, but I never wanted to be like them. All I wanted to do when I started making the Queensland sides was do my best and get selected for the next game. I never sat down and thought, 'Hmmm, the Queensland Team of the Century, I'd sure like to get picked in that!'

Playing for Australia was wonderful, because it meant you were the best in your position in the land and you wanted to win for your country. Playing for Queensland was somehow more intimate. You were busting a gut for your mates, the boys you'd played with and against for years in the local competition, and partied hard with afterwards. It was a strong bond, helped along, too, by Brisbane being a small place, in comparison with, say, Sydney where the players were far-flung – from the northern beaches to Parramatta to Randwick. Queensland blokes would smash each other in club games but rival players would generously pass on tips to each other. There was camaraderie and character about the Queensland rugby culture.

It's said often, and it may well be true, that Queensland Reds are more passionate about winning an interstate match than the New South Wales Waratahs are because we play for personal pride and they play for a Wallaby jumper. For them, in my day, an interstate game was a selection trial; for us it was an end in itself. We were saying, 'Our *job* is to beat NSW – because we are Queensland. And if we get selected to play for Australia, that's a bonus.' Whereas their thing was, 'Our mission is to get selected for Australia and if we beat Queensland in the meantime – well, that's good.' And that's the way it was.

Also, until the last couple of decades, we were usually beaten by New South Wales. That succeeded in creating a persecution complex, a siege mentality, and there was a measure of revenge in our intensity every time we took New South Wales on.

Back when I was first selected for Queensland in 1987, Bob Templeton was the coach. Tempo was a massive influence on Queensland rugby because he'd been a part of the scene for so long that he engendered a continuity and epitomised the ethos of everybody being together. And it was people like him and Johnny Breen, the manager in those days, who helped instil our pride.

Rod Macqueen, when he was coaching the Wallabies, often spoke about the 'we' not the 'me'. Which applies to everything in life, be it football, business, family or the police force. He was talking about being part of the team, working for the team, and putting back more than you take out.

Alan Jones, the broadcaster and former Wallaby coach, knew how to motivate Queenslanders. Often he'd speak to us before games, and I was astonished at the power his words had over me. He was a revelation. He'd come on like Winston Churchill: very eloquent, powerful and psychological. He made you feel 10 foot tall. His carefully crafted speeches, ending in a crescendo, that covered in minute detail our strengths and weaknesses and those of our opponents, were a stark change from the usual rip, tear and bust harangues we'd been used to getting from coaches.

Before our games against the Waratahs, he'd rev us up by telling us we were playing for *all* Queenslanders, and especially the battlers on the land whose only joy in life was listening on the radio to us whacking NSW. Worked every time.

Rod McCall, who packed down with me many times in the Queensland jersey, recalls how it was: 'Dan was ferocious playing for Queensland. I think he was motivated by the Australian selectors always picking the New South Welshmen McKenzie and Daly ahead of him and he wanted to prove them wrong. Especially when Daly lost form, and they stuck with him, ignoring Dan even when he was playing well.

'But Dan and the rest of us Queenslanders always did our best against the Waratahs, because we had all known each other growing up in Brisbane and it was personal that we didn't let each other down. It was a clique. A family. John Connolly made us spend so much time together we knew our teammates better than we did our own brothers. Also, we were all married and had kids about the same age, so we had that in common too. The Queensland culture became a huge part of our life. We respected each other and cared for each other. In our playing days, Crowls and I would spend more than four months a year in each other's pocket, playing, training and travelling. These days we see each other half a dozen times a year and our families catch up a couple of times a year. Dan and I, and the other players of our era have a bond. I'm not sure that bond exists to the same extent with Queenslanders in the professional era.'

We fancied our chances in the inaugural Super 12 series that began in March, 1996. We'd won the Super 10s in 1994 and '95, and since 1989 had won 83 out of 111 matches. For all the new money that had engulfed our game, you can't buy courage and spirit, and we Queensland boys knew we'd give our all whenever we played, whether we were paid or not. And this was especially the case when our opponents were from New South Wales. In fact, I think most of us would fork out our own hard-earned cash for the privilege of downing our old blue-clad enemies. The enormous and heartfelt rivalry involved in these encounters usually guaranteed a special game no matter where we played each other.

In all my time as a Red, few matches gave me more of a buzz than our April 1996 epic against the Waratahs before a Brisbane interstate record crowd of 22,296. It was an old-fashioned knock-'em-down-and-drag-'em-out encounter at Ballymore. Sweeping backline movements were rare, but high-intensity man-on-man warfare was in rich supply. The scrums, rucks, mauls and lineouts were our trenches that day. At the end of the match, which we won 15–13, there was not a man on either side who was not bloodied or bruised. It was as hard as our game gets as the two packs (ours reduced to seven men while a backrower covered for our winger Damian Smith who was sent off after 12 minutes) tore into each other from kick-off to final whistle.

At half-time, the score was 9–6 our way. When Coach Connolly finished his stirring address, along the lines of 'You have to die out there on the field rather than return to this dressing room at the end of the game as losers,' we stood in a circle and embraced.

We all went the extra mile that day. I picked up ankle and knee injuries in the second-half but there was no way I was coming off, and I was far from the only wounded bloke out there. Twenty minutes from the end, the score was still 9–6 but the Waratahs were gaining momentum. The ball shot out to their centre, Richard Tombs, who seemed likely to break clear. I raced up, dived desperately and ankle-tapped him. The crowd roared as Tombs tumbled headlong. The Reds lifted. Our forwards ripped into the near-Test strength NSW pack and smashed them. Minutes later John Eales kicked another penalty to give us a six-point lead and we hung on, somehow, until the end. Said our tight-head prop Matt Ryan later in the sheds, 'We knew we had them when

Ealesy got that penalty. We kicked and went again and we were flying into the ruck. There was a ruck midway through the second-half when four of us hit them and just demolished the ruck.' It was that kind of game.

In the dressing room afterwards, it fell to our assistant coach, Andrew Slack, to address us. He managed to gasp, 'I don't know how you blokes did what you did,' but then fell speechless with emotion. Former Queensland skipper Tony Shaw, who was there in the dressing room with old Queensland stalwarts Chris Handy, Mark Loane, Alec Evans and Anthony Herbert, said: 'It was hard. When you lose a man it's hard to sustain pressure, but your big hearts came through.' And Chris 'Buddha' Handy told a reporter from Brisbane's *Courier-Mail*, 'I rate this match as one of the most magnificent performances I have seen by a Queensland team. It was courage and guts more than skill. State pride was the basis on which the victory was built. It became a personal affront to the manhood of the Queenslanders to lie down to NSW. It was straight character. There was a job to be done and it would be done. They were not going to walk off the field until the job was completed.' Crowed 'Knuckles' Connolly, 'I wouldn't swap any of my players for Jonah Lomu!'

Sure, we were beaten by Natal in the semis of that year's Super 12s, but our classic clash with the Waratahs may well have been Queensland rugby's finest hour.

Despite our fine Super 12 form in 1996, the national selectors could find room for only four Queenslanders in the First Test side to play Wales at Ballymore in June. John Eales, Tim Horan, Garrick Morgan and David Wilson were the Red quartet. Possibly as punishment for stomping Josh Kronfeld in my last Test outing the previous year, I was relegated to the reserves bench – the Waratahs' Richard Harry got my spot – and I didn't make it onto the field in the game, which we won 56–25.

John Connolly told the boys who had been overlooked for the side, which featured a stampede of Brumbies (they'd beaten us by one point in our Super 12 match), to keep our heads up and keep playing so well that the selectors wouldn't be able to ignore our claims for long. Former Queensland players were ropable at what they considered the shabby treatment the Wallaby selectors had dealt to us. 'Dan Crowley and Michael Foley are the best players in their positions in Australia,' griped Rod McCall to journalist Andrew Dawson. 'I've played with Michael and Dan and I know how good they are. I know Richard Harry and Marco Caputo have improved, but I see them as investments for the future. In a year or two with Tests under their belt they may be the best. But right now Dan Crowley is the No. 1. Foley has improved to the point where he is the best hooker in Australia.'

Legendary Queensland prop Stan Pilecki had a theory why our Test representation was so small. He reckoned to get a good showing it was never enough just to beat NSW, we had to thrash them by 20 or 30 points. 'The selectors only need one opportunity to drop a Queenslander,' he declared. 'It should not be that way, but it always has been like that.'

I missed the run-on team again for the Second Test against Wales, but replaced Ewen McKenzie during our 42–3 rout of the once-formidable Welshmen, and kept my position in the cakewalk against Canada the following week when we won 74–9 and Matt Burke's 39 points, made up from three tries, nine conversions and two penalty goals, set a new Australian point-scoring record. (Another notable – rather more painful – memory I have of this match is when John Eales, who has huge feet, landed on my foot after jumping in the first lineout of the game and snapped my little toe. I finished the match in agony.)

By now, the selectors had seen the error of their ways and there were seven Queenslanders in the side, and a good thing too, because the following week we had to face the might of the All Blacks in Wellington in the inaugural Tri-Nations Test.

I've always believed a tough match is better preparation for an important game than dealing out a flogging such as we did to the Welsh and Canadians. There was no doubt we were underdone and ill-prepared to face a team that boasted Cullen, Wilson, Little, Bunce, Lomu, Mehrtens, Marshall, the Brooke brothers, Jones, Kronfeld, Brown, Fitzpatrick and Dowd. Bottom line: they gave us the father of a hiding, 43–6, on a day of driving wind and torrential rain.

As often happens, defeat, and the knowledge that some of us were on our last chance, galvanised our team and, defying all the critics, we beat South Africa in Sydney just seven days after our miserable Wellington performance. This match, which we won 21–16, was the game in which George Gregan established himself as the regular Wallaby halfback.

Talk about earning our money. Two weeks later we were back facing the All Blacks. The weather was much more conducive to rugby, but sadly the result was the same for this game, which I missed after my broken toe failed to heal. They got us again, this time 32–25. We were greatly improved from our previous effort against Fitzpatrick and Co, and with 25 minutes left on the clock looked to hold an unassailable lead of 22–9. With a minute to go, the All Blacks had pegged us back and the score stood locked at 25–25. Then a scrum packed, and their rugged centre Frank Bunce scored the winning try. It was a just reward for Frank, for earlier in this match, our breakaway, Michael Brial, had launched a furious fistic assault on the All Black, who stood his ground.

Our initial Tri-Nations foray ended dismally, with just one win from four matches, when we were beaten by the Springboks, 25–19 in a stop-start, penalty-ridden, one try apiece match in Bloemfontein in August. TV broadcaster Gordon Bray named me his Man of the Match: 'Despite conceding 13 kilograms to his opponent Bali Swart, "Dangerous Dan" epitomised the fighting spirit of the Australians. The Springboks targeted the Wallaby scrum. But the home side was frustrated by the grim resistance of our front three, and the stable platform proved a huge bonus for the Aussie backs. Crowley's workrate was exceptional. Even for a man whose aggression has never been doubted, his grand tackling around the fringes was heroic.'

I thought I'd played well in spite of carrying a broken toe throughout our campaign. All things considered, I enjoyed my first year playing with new Wallaby coach Greg Smith, who, tragically and shockingly, would soon die of a brain tumour. The New South Welshman appreciated commitment and workrate and was tough and demanding. He reckoned we weren't mentally or physically tough enough and to get us where he wanted us he'd bash us at training, trying to take us from zero to 100 in no time flat. His training sessions were hellish and I have to say they angered a lot of the boys, who believed that the flogging we were getting at training was making us flat and leg-weary in games.

Injuries, including damage to my pubis symphysis – the section where the pubic bones meet just above the genitals – kept me off the field for the rest of the season and when the Wallaby team to tour Italy, Ireland, Scotland and Wales was announced in October, I was selected, only to fail the medical. My broken toe just wouldn't heal. Coach Greg Smith had a 'no train, no play' rule. So before I trained or played the medics would give me painkilling injections all around the fracture and then another two in my back to block the nerve at the back of my toe. I was getting seven lots of needles a week, every time I trained or played. My toe was continually swollen and I had to cut the end off my sandshoe just to walk around. The needles helped, and I had no choice but to get used to it or not play. It had taken long enough to get in this team so I wanted to stay there.

Of course, all this was doing my toe no good at all and I was sidelined. I went to Brett Robinson, a Souths teammate and doctor, and he had a look at my toe and said: 'Dan, what you've got is a non-union fracture. It's not going to get better.' I took what Brett said on board but did nothing about it. Then I saw our team doctor, John Best, and he basically repeated what Brett had said: 'Mate, it's a non-union. The toe's buggered.' I asked him what could we do, and he sent me to see a specialist, Dr Peter Myers. Peter loves any code of football and is the John Eales of his profession. He said that if anything was to be done it had to be done now because the Wallabies had a break before we went on tour. 'You've got two options. One, we can go in there and open up the toe, and grind a little bit off the end of both sides which will hopefully get it to grow again and then we can stick a rod down your toe and try to join it all together again, but there's a good chance it won't work and you'd be out of the tour. Or . . . you could do what I'd do if I was you.' 'What's that?' I said. 'Cut it off,' Doc Myers replied. 'You don't need it. You won't even miss it. We'll just cut it off at the first joint and flap it over and Bob's your uncle. And you'll be right to tour.' It was a no-brainer. I went into hospital the following day. Doc Myers is a bit of a prankster. When he was putting me under the anaesthetic he started telling me a joke. Then when I woke up afterward in the recovery ward he gave me the punchline as if nothing had taken place in between. Then I looked down and I was minus my toe.

I may well have been eligible for selection in the Wallabies. But as well as my wounded toe, there was also my crook shoulder to consider – I'd damaged tendons and had 10 bone fragments floating about in it – which would need an operation at some stage. And my damaged pelvis. I turned up for the medical examination even though I, and everyone else, knew I was in doubt. The tour manager, Johnny McKay, had a go at me because he reckoned I was always turning up for medicals, getting my tour gear, then keeping it when injury ruled me out. And that's exactly what I did again this time.

The tour doctor told me that my toe had become infected, so they had to chop the remaining stub down to the next joint. Bye bye, tour. Said my front-row mate Michael Foley, who was selected in the Wallabies: 'To put into perspective what the loss of Dan means to the team, a number of things must be considered. Dan is still the only prop in the squad to have played Test-match rugby on both sides of the scrum. This invaluable experience, coupled with an outstanding, high workrate and mental and physical toughness, have made him integral to any success enjoyed in recent times by not only the Australians but more obviously the Queensland team. The entire Wallaby squad has thrown its support behind Dan and wish him a speedy recovery.' My pubis symphysis was also giving me hell. I couldn't even pick up the dog's water bucket. To try to get it right I had cortisone injections, right into my pubic bone, and they hurt like hell.

After all that, I *did* make the tour. What happened was that coach Greg Smith was hammering the boys mercilessly at training, absolutely smashing them, and a lot of the blokes got injured and couldn't play in the tour games. They beat Italy, but ranks were thin by the time they had to face Scotland at Murrayfield. I watched the match from home on TV in the middle of the night. This was about three weeks after I had my toe lopped. Australia won and I went to bed. Before dawn, the phone rang. It was Greg Smith. I said, 'Hi'. He replied, 'Ahhh, how's the toe going?' I told him, 'Fine, no problem. It's feeling better. I can move around freely now.' Said Greg: 'Well, that's good news, because Dick Harry has broken his thumb and we need you to come over and play. Can you make it?' I could.

There was a lighter side to it all when a Queensland fan, HG O'Brian, expressing his perception that an anti-Red and pro-Waratah bias still existed in Wallaby selections, wrote to a newspaper that he was amazed Greg Smith asked a Queenslander to replace Richard Harry. 'I guess he must have lost the phone number of the Randwick third-grade [prop] . . .'

I always got on well with Greg, maybe because I was one of the older guys. We could sit and chat amiably. This wasn't the case with some of the blokes, who felt he was too irascible. A lot of people said Greg's crotchety nature was caused by the fatal tumour that was, even then, forming in his brain.

I was thrown straight into the Test team to play Ireland at Lansdowne Road, Dublin, and then a week later I packed down against Wales at Cardiff. Both teams, I'm glad to say, played better and more spirited football than in their last outings against us, and we had to work hard to beat them, 22–12 and 28–19 respectively. We then beat the Barbarians to finish the tour with 12 wins from 12 games. (In London, the Queen apparently reminisced to David Campese about how I'd thrown her a flick pass with the Fourex football back at the '91 World Cup.)

It was a dream tour. I got through the Ireland game even though I'd hardly run in the eight weeks since I first had my toe operated on. Not surprisingly, I slightly strained a hamstring. That meant I couldn't train for the Wales match the following week, but because we were so low on troops I got picked anyway. I was OK for our light training-run for the wind-up match against the Barbarians in London and was selected. So I played two Tests and a game against the Baa-Baas and only had to put in one training session. Happy days.

I believed we'd evolved into a much better team than we were when we'd been battered by the All Blacks just months before. It was a wonderful end to an incident-packed and hectic season.

* * *

Life without my little toe? I've been walking in circles ever since. But seriously, in the scheme of things, losing a toe was no big deal. I've had major back problems caused by stress fractures, a hernia, a fractured sternum, a fractured ankle, numerous broken noses and head stitches. These injuries are par for the course for any forward plying his craft over many years against tough opposition. The most bizarre injury I had was one I didn't even know I'd sustained. Years back, around 1985 when I was playing rugby league in Gympie, I got tackled and hurt my shoulder when I crashed to the ground. I went to Gympie Hospital to be X-rayed and the doctors there told me there was no damage done and I'd be fine. But my shoulder was so sore I had major physiotherapy on it. Eventually the pain went away, but it took months. Ten years later, in 1996, my shoulder started causing me pain again when I was using it vigorously, so I went to hospital for an MRI. The doctor looked at the X-ray and said, 'Dan, when did you break your arm?' I told him I'd never broken my arm. My wrist, yes, but not my arm. 'Then have a look at this X-ray,' said the doctor. I did and there it was: a clear break in the bone just below the joint where the arm meets the shoulder. All those years and I didn't know I'd broken my arm back in Gympie. I had two chromoplastids (where they shave out the internal part of the shoulder socket and shave the ball of the arm bone that fits inside) to give me more freedom of movement and to reduce the pain caused by the fracture. So, a word of warning: beware the country X-ray ward!

Since school footy days, I'd lived by the rule that any player worth his salt stands up for his teammates. One Saturday night at the Sydney Football Stadium in April, 1997, I put my belief into practice and triggered the most infamous incident in my career.

Queensland was playing NSW in a Super 12 match and I admit I went into the game fired up. I always did when we played the Waratahs. We won fairly easily, 26–16, but the convincing nature of our win wasn't what caused the furore that raged for the next few days. Rather, it was the brawling that ensued. It was on for young and old from the outset, but proceedings really heated up in the second-half. Referee Wayne Erickson sin-binned our five-eighth Elton Flatley and breakaway David Wilson, which left us with 13 men for a period. Mark Connors was also despatched to the bin after Wilson and Flatley had returned. Our replacement hooker, the young Brendan Cannon, was in strife for stomping NSW winger Alistair Murdoch, and their prop Richard Harry was penalised for kneeing Flatley.

But the most infamous passage of play, the one still remembered today, ensued in the first-half when, I believed, Waratah breakaway Michael Brial stomped on our second rower Matt Cockbain. It was an ugly incident, and one that demanded retribution. Brial and I were in back play when I attacked him. I punched him repeatedly in the head, bloodying him. Brial was defenceless against my blows. He'd crossed the line and had to be dealt with. My job was to enforce the time-honoured credo of 'You start it, we finish it.'

Dazed and bleeding, he was taken from the field for treatment, but returned later. Referee Erickson missed the incident but the touch judge saw it, and, as Erickson gave me a tongue-lashing and the New South Welshmen abused me, the crowd roared. The atmosphere was electric.

All that was sensational enough, but the controversy went into overdrive at the half-time break and then again after the game ended. As we left the field, there was a bit of push and shove between Brial and me and he gave me a mouthful. After the match I headed straight for the NSW dressing room to check on Brial's condition. I'd heard he was being tended to by a doctor. We had never really been close mates, but he was a fellow Wallaby and I've always believed in the old rugby ethos that what happens on the field stays on the field, and any atrocities committed in anger out on the paddock can be made up for later with a handshake, a beer and a laugh. But Brial was in no mood to forgive me. He was still very upset about what had happened to him and he rejected my offer of a handshake and told me where to go. I responded in kind, then a couple of NSW boys chipped in and gave me a verbal spray. Their Timmy Gavin, to his credit, told me not to worry about it, everything would be OK, and I left the NSW room and returned to the Queensland sheds to celebrate our win.

That was when Waratahs' coach Matt Williams involved himself. He claimed to reporters that I had gone into the NSW dressing room determined to continue the altercation with Brial by taunting him. 'Crowley came into the change room, and he said he wanted to carry it on,' said Williams. 'It was a totally disgraceful performance and we had to kick him out.' That was garbage, and Williams knew it. I entered their room in good faith, with only honourable intentions in mind.

There followed a rash of citings, by the independent citing commissioner, Dennis Wheelahan, and officials of both teams. Wheelahan cited me, Brendan Cannon and

Richard Harry. We then cited Brial, for stomping Cockbain, Fili Finau and Richard Tombs.

I couldn't help feeling that the mass citings were a result of an over-zealous rugby hierarchy trying to sanitise rugby for all the new TV viewers that the game had won in the first flush of the professional era. I thought they were worrying needlessly and was concerned that if the blood and thunder was eradicated from our game we'd be left with a much less exciting, less emotional one. Before I fronted up to receive my punishment at the judiciary office in North Sydney on the Sunday after the match, I mused to reporters that the video age would have ruined the traditional Queensland–NSW bloodbaths of earlier decades. 'There would have been no one left on the field,' I said. 'What do they want us to do now? Go out there and play pat a cake, pat a cake, baker's man?'

Brial, Finau and Tombs all escaped suspension. Not so me, who received two weeks; Harry, who was outed for three weeks; and Cannon, recipient of a savage 15-week banishment. Brendan's sentence was the heaviest ever handed to an Australian player at interstate, provincial or Test level.

The media went crazy, and condemned the perceived thuggery. TV commentator Gordon Bray, not usually one to overreact, bordered, I thought, on the hysterical in his column in Sydney's *Daily Telegraph*:

Final word on rugby's night of shame between NSW and Queensland last weekend. During the Great War of 1914–18, a New Zealand footballer made these comments from a battlefield in Europe, 'The Australians are among the finest fighters in the world. There is nothing like them in a bayonet charge. They are fiercely impetuous. They are irresistible.' After watching Dan Crowley's performance from the commentary box last Saturday night, I was immediately reminded of the aforementioned quote. He led the bayonet charge, fought tooth and nail to defend his plot, and was fiercely impetuous. However, that's where any parallel glorification of the ANZAC ideal ends abruptly. The NSW–Queensland clash was not a life and death battle. It was a sporting contest. To a large extent, between mates. So what went wrong?

Crowley's raw aggression had two prongs: one that inspired the Reds to heroic deeds, and the other that had a sledgehammer effect on the Blues. As John Eales remarked on Channel Seven's Sportworld *last Sunday, 'He's a tough man and I'm glad he was on our side.'*

Regardless of the merit of Crowley's retaliation claim as justification for his attack on Michael Brial (a charge of stomping against Brial was subsequently dismissed), the venom of his fistic assault to the head of the unprepared NSW flanker was deplorable. To me it looked like a blatant act of thuggery.

Why then was his punishment only two weeks? The suspension actually translates to just one match. Because the Reds have this weekend off. Because the incident occurred well off the ball, it was naturally missed by the referee but reported by touch judge Micheal Keogh. I believe the system fell down at that point because the severity of Crowley's attack on Brial was not communicated to referee Wayne Erickson. The Queensland prop should have been given instant dismissal.

Dan Crowley is a fantastic competitor and a very

skilful prop. He has been a grand campaigner for state and country. However, the nature of his fiercely impetuous behaviour last Saturday night can never be condoned. It may have been appropriate on the battlefields of Europe but not in a sporting showpiece attended by 30,000 fans and seen by millions around the globe.

The bottom line must always be the safety of the players. To that end I believe his lenient punishment is a travesty of justice. Two weeks for one punch may be appropriate. But four deliberate and obvious blows to an opponent's head, the latter with full bodyweight behind his left forearm, and all with the potential to cause brain damage, in my opinion is every bit as bad as stomping on someone's head.

We played the Waratahs in a return fixture at Ballymore in June and beat them again. I was hampered in that game by groin and hamstring injuries that ended my season soon afterwards, costing me three Tests against New Zealand, two each against France, England, South Africa and Argentina, and one against Scotland, as well other internationals on the Wallabies' tour of Argentina, England and Scotland. The Queensland–NSW Super 12 game was a tame affair with none of the hostilities of the first clash. Michael Brial and I left each other alone. Oddly enough, I've bumped into Michael a few times since the incident, and have offered to make peace but, disappointingly, he seems to continue to hold a grudge.

Not so my old head-kicking mate Peter Clohessy, who played with the Reds that year in a bid to escape suspension back home in Ireland. It was a pleasure playing with the veteran hardman, and it was fun after-hours too. Peter loved a beer and a smoke and had never been a great trainer, but he enriched any side he played in, even if he incurred the wrath of referees from Lansdowne Road to Ballymore. He was a deadset dinosaur from rugby's old school. My type of bloke. Yes, he'd kicked me in that roughhouse against Munster in Cork in 1992, but all's fair in love and rugby and he was lucky he got me before I got him.

11

ON TOP OF THE WORLD

I BEGAN SEASON 1998 as I'd finished '97. In trouble.

Queensland were playing the New Zealand side Canterbury in a Super 12 clash at Ballymore in mid-March. A maul formed in the second-half, and my right arm came into contact with their flanker Angus Gardner's face. There was really nothing in it. It was just a heat-of-the-moment swinging arm, and something that happens to most forwards a few times a game. Gardner had to leave the field, but neither the referee nor the touch judges considered anything illegal had occurred. The match commissioner, however, had a different opinion and cited me for foul play. He claimed I'd attacked Gardner's head.

Plenty of pundits on both sides of the Tasman reacted by calling me a throwback to another era and stated that I deserved a hefty suspension of five weeks or more. True enough, my record wasn't good, and memories of my clash

217

with Michael Brial were still fresh. Also, the Gardner incident was played again and again on television at a time when the image-conscious powers that be were trumpeting that illegal play had no place in rugby and would be stamped out.

I argued at the judiciary hearing that I had been trying to knock the ball from Gardner's grasp but somehow my arm had connected with his face. I swore that it was an accident. The judiciary panel accepted that I didn't intend to hit Gardner's face, but still suspended me for three weeks for being reckless.

A few reporters, New Zealand and Australian, wrote that I'd got off too lightly and worried that the judiciary's 'leniency' would lead to an escalation of illegal play in the Super 12s. The Kiwis reckoned, too, that Australians were usually given light sentences in comparison with the heftier penalties dealt to their own blokes, such as serial transgressor Richard Loe, in the past. News of Brendan Cannon's recent 15-week suspension must have passed them by.

Maybe the Queensland Rugby Union was reading what these scribes put in their newspaper columns because, just as I'd passed the milestone of playing a century of games for the Reds, they decided not to pay me for the three matches I'd missed due to my suspension. This cost me a total of around $10,000, and that rankled. Queensland Rugby Union executive director Steve Thornton said, 'We looked at the situation after Dan was suspended and obviously he had to forgo match payments.' Thornton said I'd been penalised a 'small and reasonable' amount and the decision was final. I disagreed. My contract with the Queensland and Australian bodies stipulated that I could be docked match payments if

I was suspended, but gave me the right to challenge the ruling. This right was being denied to me. Thornton fired back that the decision to fine me had been made on a 'case by case' basis, and to me that smacked of persecution, so I took my case to the Rugby Union Players Association. Association spokesman Tony Dempsey ruled that 'unless a player was an habitual offender and frequently out of the game for showing disregard for the laws of the game' then he shouldn't be fined. Yes, this was my fourth suspension in seven years, but to me that didn't constitute being an habitual offender and, besides, the 'offence' for which I was being punished this time had been deemed by the judiciary to be merely reckless, not maliciously illegal.

The Rugby Union Players Association's lawyers dusted off the Industrial Relations Act to see whether my penalty was 'harsh and unconscionable'. After haggling back and forth, the Queensland Rugby Union decided that because I was still required to train for Queensland and honour my sponsorship responsibilities, it was fair that the fine was downgraded to half the original amount.

In 1998, I turned 33, but I had never enjoyed my rugby so much. Shifting to loose head in 1993 had extended my career and left me free to tear about all over the field, combining the tough, tight stuff with running the ball and setting up supports. The game had changed from the days when huge blokes who did nothing but ruck, maul and bash ruled, and when, as Bob Dwyer told me, a good big rock always beats a good little rock. No longer did backs and forwards operate exclusively as separate units. Now they were combining in attack and because, in spite of getting older,

I had retained my speed, and my ball skills and tackling technique were still in place. I was in my element.

After the early-season unpleasantness died down, I found myself, after missing all the 1997 Tests, a regular again in the Wallaby squad under new coach, Rod Macqueen. Macqueen put us into camp at Caloundra on the Sunshine Coast and instilled in us a hard-headed, professional attitude. We adopted a more scientific attack and there was a new emphasis on defence. We were a happy bunch and that was reflected in our consistently good performances on the field. For me, being a bit of a control freak, Macqueen's meticulous planning felt comfortable, and I played 10 of the next 11 Tests.

I believe Australian rugby came into its own in '98, and that watershed year of wonderful wins against the best teams in the world (only South Africa had the wood on us) laid the platform for our World Cup victory the following year and our dominance right up to the 2003 World Cup. Consider . . .

In the first Test of the year we took on England at Suncorp Stadium and thrashed them 76–0. Yes, I know that the Poms fielded a team of unknown rookies after 14 senior players pulled out following a contract dispute between their clubs and England's ruling body, but you can only beat the blokes who go up against you and we played wonderful rugby as Steve Larkham ran riot against his opposite number, 19-year-old Jonny Wilkinson, and Ben Tune and Tim Horan were unstoppable.

It's interesting to note that while most of the English players were unknown when they ran on the field that June day, within a couple of years some were household names and the backbone of an England team that won the World

Cup. Wilkinson, Danny Grewcock and Phil Vickery, not forgetting coach Clive Woodward, have said since that the shame of that massive defeat in Brisbane showed them what international rugby was all about and made them vow never to suffer such a thrashing again.

A week later, we handed a 45–3 walloping to a full-strength Scotland in Sydney and repeated the dose at Ballymore, 33–11. Larkham was again majestic at five-eighth, Joe Roff was a powerhouse and Ben Tune once more made plenty of ground on the wing, scoring his sixth try in three Tests. I was a reserve for those three games, but got onto the paddock in each and did my bit.

In July, in the first Tri-Nation Test of the season, we lined up against New Zealand at the Melbourne Cricket Ground. In spite of our form against the Northern Hemisphere touring sides, few gave us much chance of wresting the Bledisloe Cup from the All Blacks after their white-hot form of the previous year. In fact, at that point we'd racked up seven successive losses to them, stretching back to 1994. Such pessimism did not extend to the team. We knew we were turning into a formidable force, and the All Blacks were going through a period of transition with Jonah Lomu's form affected by illness, and the retirement of the formidable trio of Frank Bunce, Zinzan Brooke and Sean Fitzpatrick, who'd been supplanted as skipper by Tane Randell.

Although I was a reserve, the tip was that I'd be brought on at half-time. *Courier-Mail* rugby writer Andrew Dawson noted in the lead-up to the Test:

Wallaby enforcer Dan Crowley is poised for an early entry into Saturday's clash as Australia look to find the spark to ignite them to a rare victory against New Zealand, Crowley, a rough and tumble prop, could be called from the bench to start the second half . . . His aggression, leadership and mobility have muscled him towards extended playing time. He backs down to no one and is a natural leader and an encouraging talker, qualities missing from the starting front row. Richard Harry and fellow prop Andrew Blades are quiet on the field, while hooker Phil Kearns does not command the presence he once did.

Crowley is one of the few props in world rugby who can back up what he preaches. He is relentless around the field, whether carting the ball forward, contributing to phase play, or making desperate, lunging tackles. Coach Rod Macqueen seems to have deliberately underplayed Crowley's hand in the opening three Tests of the season, giving him only limited playing time. Macqueen seemingly had wanted him fresh when it counted – in the Tri-Nations series.

There is a fantastic atmosphere at the MCG. When we did our ritual walk around the ground and warm-up on the Friday before the Saturday Test, I got tingles up my spine. There was no one there but us pretty much, just cleaners and a few blokes putting the advertising marks onto the field while we went through our paces. As a youngster I'd been a huge cricket fan and the MCG was a shrine. I strolled out onto the field before the other guys came out of the sheds and just took it all in, looked up at those vast stands, and thought, 'Wouldn't this be a lonely place to be if you dropped a catch or got out for a duck in a Test match!'

We beat New Zealand 24–16 in that first Test. I entered

the fray in the 13th minute after Richard Harry damaged his kneecap. All our points came from Matt Burke. Afterwards, captain John Eales interrupted our wild celebrations when he gathered us in a huddle and told us not to get carried away with the win. We had only won *a* Bledisloe Cup match, not the Bledisloe Cup itself. There was still plenty of work to do if we wanted to achieve that, and then go on to establish ourselves as the best team in the world.

John knew what he was talking about, because the following week in Perth we were brought down to earth by a committed South African side, who scraped home 14–13 in a grim kick-fest played in driving rain. In truth, we blew it. We were attacking in their quarter in the final minutes but kept plugging away for a try when we could have slotted a field goal. Phil Kearns was savagely stomped and needed 13 stitches in a head wound, but the Springbok culprit escaped detection. I made the run-on team that day and jealously hung on to my first-choice loose-head position for the rest of the year, leaving my main rival Richard Harry cooling his heels and waiting for me to make a slip.

It's the mark of a good team to bounce back after a loss. That's what we did when we secured the Bledisloe Cup with another win, 27–23, over New Zealand in front of their own rabid fans at Lancaster Park. We gave them a proper dusting in the forwards. Reported Peter Jenkins in *Wallaby Gold: The History of Australian Test Rugby*:

On a day when inspirational defence coupled with the go-forward of their pack was crucial to Australia's success, the highlight was an ensemble try that ranks with the finest ever scored by a Wallaby side. For three minutes and

10 seconds, shortly before half-time, Australia retained and controlled possession in a passage of play that lasted 17 rucks and one maul. Starting from a lineout win 30 metres from their own line, the Wallabies punched the ball up three times, first through halfback George Gregan, then using No. 8 Toutai Kefu and centre Daniel Herbert. Winger Jason Little, who had been brought into the side for the injured Ben Tune, injected himself into the play and made an incisive bust. On and on the Wallabies rumbled until, when close to the All Blacks' line, five-eighth Stephen Larkham took the ball on the blindside, swivelled and delivered an inside pass for Matt Burke to score.

Even so stern a critic of forwards as David Campese raved about our pack's 'mighty performance', on a ground where so many Australian sides had come to grief, and singled out John Eales, Tom Bowman, Toutai Kefu and me for praise. He lauded our 'fierce committment' and reckoned we'd made the much-vaunted New Zealand forwards look 'ordinary,' not a word you'd usually associate with the All Blacks.

That day – any day – it was great to be a Wallaby.

It's funny the things you remember. When we came out onto the field for the pre-game formalities I was standing there when a helicopter floated over our heads carrying monster New Zealand and Australian flags. There was a gale blowing and the chopper was struggling to contain the huge sheets of material that were being caught in the wind. Swinging violently back and forth less than a hundred metres directly above us, it was impossible not to get nervous. I stopped worrying about how we were going to beat the All Blacks and started thinking about where I was going to run when the helicopter crashed. I also remember my brother Michael and my sister-in-law, Vicki, were there, and after the game I did a Pat Cash and ran up into the stands to celebrate with them. Michael was really giving it to the Kiwi fans. They couldn't believe we'd taken the Bledisloe Cup from them. For the following two weeks he and Vicki travelled around New Zealand giving them stick. Is there a better way for an Aussie to holiday in New Zealand?

A second loss to the Springboks at Johannesburg's Ellis Park three weeks later took the gloss off our trans-Tasman triumph and cost us the Tri-Nations trophy. Perhaps our heads were still in the clouds after Lancaster Park, or more likely we were victims of a tremendous Springbok defence that repelled our attack the entire game. Larkham was harassed into ineffectuality and we were out-slugged in the forwards. There were some nasty elements in the crowd and we were pelted with bottles, beer cans and fruit.

Back on home soil the following Saturday night, at the Sydney Football Stadium, we continued our domination of the All Blacks. This time we bested them 19–14 in a thriller highlighted by Matt Burke's barnstorming try after a slick inside ball from Gregan. Burke was on fire in that series. We were down 14–9 at the time and the match had only about 10 minutes to go. Unfortunately for Matt, the impact when he hit the ground for his match-winning try dislocated his shoulder and tore his ligaments from the bone. He was out of action for the next six months. Knowing him, he may have reckoned it was worth it. Our Bledisloe Cup whitewash was Australia's first since 1929.

I believe that clean sweep – beating New Zealand in the Third Bledisloe Cup game when the series was already ours – was when the Wallabies got our confidence back. It was a launching pad for the unprecedented success that followed. We'd notched a win against them here and there, but the All Blacks had been dominating us for ages. Now we were thinking that we had their measure, and that gave us the self-belief to keep repeating the dose in the coming years. And not just to New Zealand, but to the other great teams in the world as well.

A fine season was wrapped up with three World Cup qualifying wins: over Fiji (66–20), a game I missed when I tore a hamstring at training; Tonga (74–0); and Western Samoa (25–13), in which I scored my first and only inter-national try. I wish I could talk about my great 50-metre run with a chip and chase, but no, I crossed the line after a 1-metre lunge at the back of a rolling maul. Australia was on target to be a major force in our game's showpiece, the World Cup, to be staged in Great Britain at the end of '99.

But first there was the small matter of a Wallaby tour to France and England. I was so up for it, because if I played well against the hardheads of England in London, and France in Paris, I'd do my World Cup chances a lot of good, but in an old, familiar story, injury dashed my hopes. I damaged my ankle at training and missed out on the trip after working so hard to cement my position.

It was a bitter blow. I thought I'd been playing good foot-ball. At first the medicos thought my ankle was only twisted. But I knew better. I have this thing where if I break a bone I have an overwhelming need to throw up, and this is just how I felt when I went over on my ankle. Still, I bowed to their superior knowledge and played on it after it began feel-ing a bit better, though my foot was sore, especially around my heel, all the next season. It wasn't until 12 months later that I discovered that I had broken a bone off in my ankle and there was a piece floating around the back of my heel.

By 1999, I was approaching the end of my career, yet I had two big goals: I wanted to be a part of that World Cup campaign and play 50 games for the Wallabies; and I had in my sights the chance of overtaking Andrew Slack's record of 133 games for the Reds.

After we beat NSW 30–13 in May, making us 4–0 (with a draw) over our traditional foe since the institution of the Super 12 series, a reporter asked me what it was that gave us the edge over a team with just as many great players. I was still fired up with emotion, and so to answer his question I grabbed the koala emblem on the front of my jersey and said, reiterating my long-held belief: 'We play for the Queensland jumper. They play for Australian jerseys. If we play well in this, the green-and-gold one will come along. But this is the jumper we play for.'

This philosophy flew in the face of the official line, touted in the poster that was printed to publicise that Super 12 clash. It was made to look like an old boxing poster with the headline 'The Scraps For Test Caps' and a series of man-on-man duels to decide who'd make the Wallaby team. There was Nathan Grey vs Tim Horan, Tiaan Strauss vs Toutai Kefu, and Richard 'Dirty' Harry vs Dan 'The Man' Crowley. This was a blatant allusion to the biffo between Michael Brial and me in 1997, and seemed like a bit of a double standard to me. The administrators bleat about violence destroying the game's image, then turn around and use it to sell tickets.

The Reds had a great Super 12 season, right up until our semi-final against the Canterbury Crusaders at Ballymore. Although it looked like a Ballymore final was ours for the taking, we were beaten by 28–22 when the Kiwis reversed their defeat from earlier in the season. To me, as I told reporters after the match, 'A great season isn't great enough.'

That loss was my 116th game for Queensland. I knew that if I could hang in there in 2000 and 2001, Andrew Slack's record could be mine for the taking. Someone asked Andrew if he was nervous as I closed in on his 133 all-time appearance record, and he first replied that as far he knew I wanted to go on playing till I was 96 – then added that since I was getting on, I'd be 36 in 2001, my injuries and ageing limbs might just save his hide.

Meanwhile, on the Wallaby front, I was picked in the First Test against Ireland at Ballymore on 7 June. I packed down against Peter Clohessy, who'd returned to his homeland after his stint with the Reds. Peter was back to his aggravating best. He stamped on Ben Tune's leg, causing an injury bad enough for the speedy and determined winger to leave the field. In that match, too, David Wilson was kicked in the head and only his headgear saved him from some serious stitching. None of which stopped me meeting up with Cloey after the game, which we won 46–10.

Clohessy's performance and the scoreline set me to thinking about how very much my game had changed since professionalism. My old mate had become a bit of an anachronism. I had finally come to realise that cheap-shot merchants and bully boys were a dying breed at Test level. The game was now way too fast to be getting involved in thuggery or squaring up to blokes. If you were preoccupied with that stuff there was no way you'd have the time to do your job. You couldn't even give away penalties anymore, let alone leave your side short by getting sent off. Attacks were so sophisticated by the late 1990s that no team could hope to win without a full complement of players. Gone, too, were the days when second rowers were clumsy giraffes picked to do nothing but jump in the lineouts and push in scrums. You took your life in your hands in some of those lineouts of old when a rival could just line you up with an elbow and bust you open. These days, no one just stood there, they were running left, right and centre before the throw, and with video refs you wouldn't get away with it anyway. The increased speed of the game had led to sides no longer committing the bulk of their pack to the breakdown, preferring instead to have the quicker forwards out reinforcing the backline, and those guys were having to think two or three phases ahead. Every player, not least the forwards, had to keep their mind focussed on the job for the full 80 minutes. That said, while the game had become cleaner and faster, both are hard in terms of physical contact.

I was talking to Cloey not long ago and we both reckoned that while it wasn't such a bad thing that the viciousness has been eliminated from rugby, a man who illegally obstructs the play deserves whatever he gets. The head is now off limits, although it's OK to rake the body. 'Christ,' Cloey reminisced, 'when we played the All Blacks, if you were standing in the shower and didn't have bleeding ruck marks all over your body you hadn't done your job on the ground. They'd hurt for a couple of days then heal up. They were part of the game. What goes around, comes around. You give as good as you get and when you get it back you cop it sweet and wait for revenge.'

In the second encounter in Perth, that June 1999, the Irish curbed their aggression, kept their minds on the task, and led us 11–9 at half-time. In the end, we only pipped them by six points, 32–26.

For the Centenary Test against England on our home soil a week after the Ireland Test, I found myself a reserve. My Reds teammate, the bulkier Glen Panaho, had taken my spot, although I did get a run from the bench. I was wondering if my World Cup spot was in jeopardy, but, as I'd always done when my position in the team was under challenge, put my head down and did the best I could. This time the English team was a different proposition from the easybeats of the year before. Jonny Wilkinson was joined by such class acts such as Jeremy Guscott, Neil Back, Richard Hill, Martin Johnson and Jason Leonard. We won 22–15, thanks to slashing tries by Ben Tune and Joe Roff, but they gave us a real run for our money.

I got into a second-half stink with rival prop Darren Garforth. He grabbed my leg in the scrum, which is a dangerous thing to do, and I let him have a flurry of lefts, one or two of which connected. Some people said I tried to finish Darren off with a headbutt but what really happened was that I lost my footing and pitched forward towards him, headfirst. But what are you supposed to do? Grabbing a prop's leg in the middle of a scrum could end with it collapsing and someone breaking their neck.

The Centenary Test was a wonderful occasion, and gave us the chance to revel in rugby tradition. At an official function on the Wednesday night before the match we were feted by all the old Wallaby captains, and before we ran onto Stadium Australia at Homebush, Alan Jones, coach of the 1984 Grand

Slam Wallabies, in a spellbinding and inspirational speech, said, 'You can do something that will be talked about in another hundred years.' In a further link with the past, we wore a replica of the jersey and crest worn by the Australian team in their first match against England at the Sydney Cricket Ground in 1899. To my horror the jersey was blue, the colour of the NSW Waratahs. Of course I wore it, I didn't have a choice, but after the game, as the Prime Minister, the Governor-General and other dignitaries hovered around us, I declared that the only reason I was still wearing the dreaded blue jumper was that I was too exhausted to take it off and, in fact, as soon as I got home I was going to cut the Wallaby crest off and stick it on a red jersey. And, on a roll, I quipped that at least tonight we had improved the Blues' win–loss record.

It was good to be part of Australia's revenge against the Springboks in our first Tri-Nations encounter, at Suncorp Stadium in July. We won 32–6 even though we were heavily outweighed and out-muscled in the forwards. The game was a triumph for our backs. Roff and Horan scored two tries apiece and Burke picked up the other. South Africa didn't cross our line.

That year the Springboks had the most formidable pack in world rugby. The week before the match, they had monstered the All Blacks. How do you attempt to take on such a pack? With a guy as big as Os du Randt, you try to take him low. In that match we did it sometimes but not often enough. Or, another way to best bigger, slower blokes, is to try for a quick strike, get in and win the ball before they have a chance to shove you off it. And you have to counter their weight by the whole front row putting pressure on them from different angles.

* * *

In an effort to improve our scrummaging, ever-innovative Rod Macqueen invited Dr Brendan Burkett, who lectured in biomechanics at the University of the Sunshine Coast, to join us at our Caloundra camp. Dr Burkett attached electronic load cells to the back of our scrum machine. The cells measured how much pressure each forward was individually exerting, as well as the power and duration of the collective shove, and relayed the information to Rod's laptop computer.

Macqueen may not have been the best coach I played under when it came to skills, strategy or the technical side of the game, but he was the best manager, and at the elite level I believe success is 90 per cent due to planning and 10 per cent coaching. Rod took the management work practices that had made him such a successful businessman and applied them to rugby. He always had a team of expert coaches, trainers, doctors, physiotherapists and sports psychologists around him, whom he pumped mercilessly for information that would make us better players and a better team.

The half-time break is exactly 10 minutes. Some coaches would just think, 'I'll take however long I can get to address the guys.' To make sure he had enough time to say what he wanted to say, Rod put the stopwatch on the players to make certain they didn't dawdle into the sheds or take a minute more than necessary to sit down and grab a drink. He timed the physios and doctors to ensure that they took absolutely not a second longer than they needed to do their work. That way, Rod knew *exactly* how much time he had to say his piece. Sometimes you see coaches out on the sideline, still trying to say things to the players when they are going back onto the field. Not Rod. He had his 5.6 minutes and he used it. And then there's the tracksuits. Wallaby fans may feel like they're missing out when they see our team taking the field in their dark-green tracksuits while the All Blacks or the Lions tear onto the field in their black or red jerseys pumped up and ready to play. But the tracksuits were Rod's method of curbing our rivals' emotion. Just as the pre-match rituals – the haka, the chanting of the Lions' huge army of fans – are sending the other side into a frenzy, we all leave the field for a minute or so to take off our trackies. The anti-climax would sap the other team of a bit of their emotion and we returned to start the game on our own terms. The stopwatch and the tracksuits were just little things, but with Rod Macqueen, little things were everything.

Macqueen gave each Wallaby a diary at the start of the season. You could turn to a date which was four months down the track and read that at 2.50 on that day you'd be boarding Qantas Flight QF5 for London. That helped us plan our lives around rugby and took away a lot of the stress.

I found myself a reserve for the match against New Zealand, a week after the Springbok match, which we lost badly, 34–15. Once more Glenn Panaho was preferred to me. It increasingly seemed part of Rod Macqueen's tactics to start a game with Panaho, who'd get through the earlier grunt work, then bring me on after half an hour for my mobility and busier workrate when the game had opened up. I understood the thinking, but, being a proud sort of bloke, I was desperate to be in that run-on team and play the entire match.

It was clear to everyone, not least me, that with the World Cup just weeks away, I may have played my last match as a Wallaby. Nor was my peace of mind improved when Australia played well in a one-point loss to the Springboks and a 28–7 thrashing of New Zealand in the games I missed. When the names of the World Cup squad were read out I had my fingers, toes and everything else crossed. And it worked – I made the team. I would play in my third World Cup. I vowed to make it a swansong to remember.

It was too, in a way. Blades and Harry got the two prop spots in the matches that mattered, but I was selected in the run-on side against the US and made it onto the field to help the boys notch big wins against Romania, Ireland (when I packed as hooker) and France in the final.

I was dropped from the bench, for Rod Moore, for the semi-final against South Africa at Twickenham. And it was all my own doing. Richard Harry had a lock on loose-head prop, and Andrew Blades a mortgage on the tight.

Although I had been a reserve in all matches, now the issue of my size, which had dogged me for a decade, was back again. We were facing the huge Springbok front row of Visagie, Drotske and du Randt. The day before the team for the semi-final was announced, Macqueen called me to his room. Getting the private call to the boss's room is never good. Alec Evans was Rod's forwards coach and his concerns that I wasn't big enough, forged back in 1982, had re-emerged. Rod asked me a simple question: 'If Blades was hurt in the first minute, could you handle du Randt?'

The Springboks were huge and excellent scrummagers, and I hadn't played tight head for some years. I knew if I lied and said yes and Andrew got hurt and I wasn't up to the task, I would be letting the team down. I was aware I was basically signing my retirement papers, so I said, 'Are you wanting me to end my career?' He said, 'No. But what if Blades got hurt?' I replied, 'Then I'd struggle.' I could have taken a gamble, but all that mattered was that the team won.

I paid the price for my honesty and was dropped from the team for the South Africa game and the semi against the All Blacks. It hurt not to play any part at all in our 27–21 victory, which was one of the most gripping games I have ever seen.

It was then that I decided to retire from Test rugby at the end of the tournament. The fact was, my body was showing the wear and tear of 14 years of top-level rugby. My shoulder was still bad and would need another operation to loosen the socket. The doctor said I had one operation left in me and then I'd have to have an artificial joint fitted. Also, I had three beautiful kids I was keen to spend more time with, and I wanted to make amends to my wife for all the years I had to be away playing for the Reds and the Wallabies. So I decided that I'd concentrate on playing as well as I could for two more years for Souths and the Reds and, of course, overtake Andrew Slack's 133 games for Queensland record.

Then, just when I thought my Wallaby career was over, I received a wonderful surprise from Coach Macqueen. He decided I was the man for the job against the French in the final. I would be on the bench, but I'd get a run at some stage. And I did. It was only 10 minutes. Blades and Harry had done the job and in some way I think it was a little bit of gratitude from Macqueen for my honesty. But hell, it was a World Cup final and I was going to enjoy every minute of it.

After the French beat the All Blacks in a helter-skelter classic the week before, many people favoured them to down us in the final at Cardiff Arms Park on 8 November. But, as it happened, the French had peaked for the All Blacks game, and the flair, enterprise and delightful passing and chip-kicking which had blown the Blacks off the park were nowhere in evidence when they faced us. They were flat and stodgy, overawed by the big occasion, and to put us off our game, they once more resorted to punching, biting, scratching, testicle-twisting, kicking and eye-gouging. They were also intent on killing the ball in mauls and rucks to stifle our attack. John Eales threatened to take us off the paddock at one stage, as a protest against their foul play. He told the referee that he feared for our safety. While they were fighting, we were taking them apart, and the final score in this scrappy, safety-first encounter was 35–12. Our stars that day were Man of the Tournament Tim Horan and the fit-again John Eales, who remained cool and kept us focussed on rugby, not retribution.

At the end of the game, my 39th and last Test, I didn't reflect for too long on my long life as a Wallaby. There would be plenty of time for that later. I joined the boys for a party to remember.

Looking back, though, while I might have seemed delighted, deep down, where it matters, I felt hollow. I didn't care what anyone told me, as a reserve I wasn't *really* part of the victory. Having been on the bench or part of the squad isn't enough to bask in the glory of the 15 guys who ran onto the paddock and won the World Cup for Australia. Some of the other outsiders lapped it up, but not me. As I celebrated there in Paris I confess I felt a bit of a fraud, and was racking my brain. Why wasn't I considered good enough to make the team? Could I have trained harder, could I have played better?

* * *

My three World Cup campaigns will always be among the most cherished memories of my time in rugby. Each tour was very different from the others. The World Cup has only fairly recently come to be considered as the game's Holy Grail, and for the 1991 tournament in the UK, which we won, we were very laidback. Yes, we desperately wanted to win the Cup, but for the pool matches it was no more intense for us than minor games on a normal Wallaby tour. We had very narrow, some would say lucky, wins over Argentina, Western Samoa and Ireland. Then, as we moved through the stages, getting closer with each win to the final, we got into it. We were saying, 'We can really win this!' By the time we played New Zealand in the semi, and then England in the final, we were ready to go.

In South Africa in 1995, the Wallabies were a team in transition, falling somewhere between 1991 and the heavy-duty intensity of 1999. The political pressure was heavy in South Africa then. It was vital for the Springboks and their fans that they do well after so long in the rugby wilderness. And because there was a lot of lawlessness in the streets of the capital cities, we had to stay in a hotel in the sticks, confined to our own floor, with a 24-hour guard. Whenever we left our quarters we had to be accompanied by an armed guard. Not much fun.

Bob Dwyer was just coming into his own as a coach then, and had some very complex strategies and plays he tried to instil in us. By 1999, these plays of Bob's were commonplace, but they were very new in '95 in South Africa and we weren't up to them. He'd get us together before training and say: 'We're going to set a scrum *here*, and I want this bloke to take the ball and get tackled *here*. Then I want you to get the ball and get tackled *here*. And you, you're to cart the ball to *here* and get tackled. Then by the time this fella gets the ball there'll be a gap because all the tacklers will have been taken out of the play.' Then we'd do it and instead of getting tackled *here*, where Bob said, the ball carrier would run to *there* where he was brought down. Bob would yell, 'Why'd you dart back in there?' And the bloke would say, 'Well, I saw a gap and reckoned I could get through.' Bob, tearing his hair, would go: 'But we *know* there's a gap there. We planned it that way. But I didn't want you to get tackled by the guy who did tackle you, because he's going to stay there where our next play is aimed. We wanted him to stay out where I *told* you to run!' The bloke would look sheepish and say: 'Oh, fine. Let's try it again.' And once more, he'd get mixed up. The boys couldn't comprehend Bob's tactics, which were three levels more complex than they'd ever been asked to put into practice.

We just didn't have the cattle to win the World Cup in '95. We simply were not strong enough to win the final and would have been beaten by whichever team, New Zealand or South Africa, made it into the decider. It transpired that it was a pumped-up South Africa.

In my last World Cup campaign, in 1999, it all came together, though by that stage of my career I was hanging on to selection in the team by my fingernails.

At the start of the 2000 season, I'd played 120 games for the Queensland Reds and I had only 14 to go to beat Andrew Slack's record. By my reckoning, if I could stay in the side throughout 2000 and Queensland made the Super 12 finals, I could become the most-capped Queenslander.

But my dream turned to dust in late February, when, after a couple of lead-up games, our coach John Connolly dropped me not only from the Queensland run-on team, but from the bench as well for the Super 12 opener against Otago with their all All Black front row of Carl Hoeft, Anton Oliver and Kees Meeuws, in Dunedin. He reckoned Panaho, fresh recruit Fletcher Dyson and the new young prop on the block, Nick Stiles, were in superior form and represented better bets for the future. After 14 seasons and 122 games for my state, I was history. 'I'm obviously disappointed, but I'm not going to get bitter and twisted about it,' I told reporters. I lied.

Being dropped from my beloved Reds left me feeling deeply let down, and so did the way in which coach John Connolly told me I was no longer part of his plans. As they say, it's not what you do, it's the way you do it, and 'Knuckles' did it very badly indeed. I was rooming with Glen Panaho on the Thursday morning prior to our first Super 12 game. Ten minutes before we boarded the bus for the ground, nature called. When I went into the bathroom, Glen was on his bed watching TV. When I came out, Glen had disappeared and had been replaced on the bed by 'Knuckles'. Being a smart-arse and knowing this man for a decade I quipped, 'Didn't I just flush you?' as I looked back to the bathroom. He didn't smile, but he did end up having the last laugh. 'Crowls,' Connolly said, 'this is the hardest decision I've had to make in my life, but we're not picking you in the team.' Then he added, 'And you're not on the bench either. You're out.' He left it like that, and walked away. What could I say?

You assume that the coach would have a fairly good

handle on the team he wanted to use for the upcoming season. I had spoken long and hard to John at the end of the World Cup about my loyalty to the Reds and that that was why I signed only a Queensland contract. I had even said no to any post-Cup holidays, opting instead for ankle and shoulder operations to ensure I hit the Super 12 running. He could have done what Brisbane Broncos rugby league coach Wayne Bennett has done in the past with long-serving players and given me a warning to make other commitments, but he didn't.

One thing about John Connolly is that he is very ruthless when it comes to football and his only concern, I now believe, was that I was around in case Stiles didn't measure up early on or Panaho got injured and he could use me in an emergency. 'Knuckles' didn't care about the position he had put me in. He had done the same thing to Rod McCall a few seasons before, so I shouldn't have been that surprised.

I was humiliated and angry, but determined not to let my feelings show. When the names of the players who had made the side were read out I was the first to walk over to Nick Stiles, who'd taken my spot, and say, 'Congrats, mate, well done.' Nick was a Souths junior. I knew him and his family well, and they are great people.

My record over many years showed that I could take being dropped if I wasn't playing well or my rivals were in better form, but I was playing well then and certainly none of the other props on offer were performing any better individually; nor was the scrum looking as solid as previous years. I have a lot of respect for Stiles but my being dropped like that just wasn't right. Connolly refused to reconsider his decision. He told me, 'I've made it and I'm sticking with it.'

So, I played only another two games for the Reds in 2000. At season's end I didn't hang around, even though I had another year to run on my Queensland contract, a year when I could have sat back and been paid good and easy money. I sought a release from my final year to take up a contract with Leeds Tykes in the English second division competition and to see a little of the world with my family. The deal was that they wanted me for three years but I'd sign for one and extend if I wanted to, with the chance of a coaching job at the end if everything worked out well. The money was OK, and the hierarchy there won me over when they told me they had a lot of promising young players.

The boys at Leeds were all really good guys, but my heart just wasn't in it. I had no history with the club and I found I had nothing to play for. Of course, I wanted to win, but that's not always enough. I have to *believe* in the cause to give 100 per cent. My problem is that I had an amateur mentality while playing a game that had become professional. Just money or notching another couple of competition points are not enough reason for me to take my intensity to the highest level. I know a lot of players, such as Tim Horan, David Campese, David Wilson and Michael Lynagh, who have had successful stints overseas at the end of their Australian careers, but I don't think any of them approached their Wallaby or state form.

Then my father got sick, so my family and I left Leeds and returned to Brisbane. I haven't made a better decision in my life. Dad pulled through, but he is still unwell today. His problem was a bad heart, which couldn't be operated on because of emphysema caused by a lifetime of smoking. He doesn't whinge or blame anyone. Like any good footballer, he just keeps on playing the game.

12

NO REGRETS

As I near my 40th year, I know that I probably have fewer years in front of me than I have behind me. Reflecting on my life, I realise that I never had concrete goals from the beginning; I just formulated them as I went along and tried to attain them with passion. My father once told me something about work which I have never forgotten: 'Dan, it doesn't matter what you do in life, make sure you enjoy it, as you'll be doing it a long time.' And I've always followed his words of wisdom, in my family life, my football and police careers.

However, if Peggy Doyle had had her way, I would never have become a policeman. As Mum and Dad's sponsor when they started a new life in Australia, and a pioneering business-woman, Peggy, who has long since passed away, knew me from birth. She was one of my referees when I joined the police. 'Mrs Doyle, as Dan's referee can you outline why you believe he would be a suitable candidate for the Queensland

Police?' the recruitment officer asked. 'I can't,' was Peggy's stern reply. Thinking that he had found a skeleton in my closet, some heinous event in my past, the officer inquired further. 'OK, what has Dan done wrong that you believe would preclude him?' Said Peggy, 'Nothing is wrong with Dan, my dear fellow. It's *you*. I think he can do far better for himself in business than with the police, and I have told him so.'

Maybe in the long run she was right, but for all the service's faults I wouldn't have passed up the enriching, thrilling and maturing experiences that being a police officer provided. I met a number of good hardworking men and women along the way, though a number of lazy ones as well. The police service has changed a lot in the decade since I have left, completely for the better. But now having had a taste of private enterprise, I realise they have a way to go . . .

Staying close to what I know, I now run a commercial investigation business, Verifact. We don't investigate those seedy mum versus dad domestic matters. We concentrate on work for federal and state government organisations, insurance companies and large public and private corporations. When I left the police I started my company humbly, operating out of my back garage. Now Verifact operates nationally. It isn't Microsoft, but, hey, it's a living and one I feel comfortable with and am pursuing with enthusiasm.

I am still involved in rugby, but only on the fringes. I like it that way. When I finished playing, many people asked me, 'Will you take up coaching?' I couldn't get the word 'No' out quick enough. Not coaching fair-dinkum football, anyway. I may try my hand coaching junior football a bit later in life. To be a top-line coach today you have to be obsessed, consumed, a fanatic. The last thing I would want to be doing is poring over endless video replays to find that elusive something, that chink in the opposition's armour. Give me a strategic business plan any day.

I was involved for four years as the players' delegate on the Australian Rugby Union board and that opened my eyes to the realisation that if I wanted to make a difference to rugby it would be as an administrator, not as a coach. I am fortunate still to be involved in the game through TV.

Currently, I have the great fortune of working with Gordon Bray and Tim Horan as a member of the Channel Seven commentary team for the Test matches. Yet, I quickly found that the world of TV is very much like rugby: you are only as good as your last game. I was left in no doubt about this in my first meeting with David Leckie, the Channel Seven CEO. David, not one to mince words, put it simply: 'Dan, good to have you on board, you've been doing well. Keep improving and we'll keep you going. If you don't, we'll piss you off.' Even *I* could work out that criteria.

It is great still to be involved in rugby through the commentary, but difficult in that sometimes you have to comment negatively on old teammates' Australian performances. I didn't like being criticised by my peers in the commentary box when I was playing but I knew if I was honest with myself most of the negative remarks were close to the mark. I try to be objective and honest and I realise I can never hope to make everyone happy. When I first started with Seven, my old friend Brendan Cannon rang and complained: 'What's the go with you bagging me during yesterday's game? We're supposed to be mates and you put shit on me!' I replied: 'Hold on. I didn't put shit on you. I said that you weren't playing as well as I know you can. Did you hear me say how hard it is to get your heart rate down to steady yourself for a lineout throw?' I told him that if I didn't speak the truth the public would know and my credibility would be shot. We ended the conversation still as mates with my parting words: 'Play a blinder this week and give me something to give you a wrap about.' No thanks to me, Brendan did play a blinder and has been one of Australia's best ever since.

One of the things I like about doing television commentary is that it takes me out of my comfort zone. I am not used to it, it's difficult, and we all need to be stretched once in a while.

Where do I go from here? To tell you the truth, I'm not really sure. Is anyone *ever* sure? I'll work hard to build my business and look at a venture or two on the side if opportunity knocks. I suppose my next biggest goal that has arisen along the way is my family. The past 40 years have been about me: What was I trying to achieve? What did I want to do? Where was I going? Now with our children growing at a rate of knots, the focus is changing to what do *they* want to do? Where do *they* want to go? What do *they* want to be? Hopefully, I'll help them to achieve what they can and be the best they can be at what they want to do.

My mum and dad, like many others of their generation, took a bold step and moved across the world to start a new and better life for them and their family. It is only now as I get older that I am beginning to fully appreciate the many wonderful things they have done to help me to succeed; the unbelievable sacrifices they made through their lives to ensure that my brothers and I never went without. If I can be half the parent to my children Mum and Dad have been to me, I know I will have succeeded in realising my parenting goal, that's for sure.

About my wife . . . well, what can I say? She has stuck by me through thick and thin, since I was a teenager. How can you truly appreciate the work that your partner in life does for you? While I travelled the world playing in front of huge crowds and meeting famous people, she was at home ensuring that everything was in proper working order. She has lived through the highs and lows of my sporting career, and the down and dangerous times in the police service. All the while we've grown closer together. She has always been there with a supportive word and a grab of the hand, and also the odd clip across the head combined with a well-timed 'Idiot!' to bring me back to earth. I am severely in the red when it comes to showing her love and attention, and my future will be dedicated to correcting the imbalance.

The cricket legend Steve Waugh speaks of a sign they placed above the exit of the Australian team's tour bus: 'No regrets'. It meant do the very best you can, so that in later years when you ponder your successes and failures you can be truly satisfied in the deepest part of your heart with your life. I was never the greatest star to grace the rugby paddock, and I'm sure there have been better policemen, but I know in the deepest part of *my* heart that I always did my best. I have no regrets.